MARKETING
A Financial Approach

H. Peeru Mohamed

Kaveri Books
New Delhi - 110 002

Edition 2015
ISBN: 81-7479-010-1

Published by
Kaveri Books
4832/24, Ansari Road
New Delhi-110002 (India)
Tel: 011-23288140, 23245799
E-mail : info@kaveribooks.com
kaveribooks@gmail.com
Website: www.kaveribooks.com

Typeset at
Delta Book World, New Delhi - 110 002.

PRINTED IN INDIA

MY FATHER

Preface

In view of the growing competitive pressures, the challenges faced by marketing professionals are consistently increasing. As such strategic marketing decision making becomes more complex and risky. To face this situation meaning fully and to win the game marketers have to equip themselves with all those functional areas which have close linkage with the functions of marketing. Undoubtedly "finance" is one such functional area.

The nature of inter face between finance and marketing functions compels marketers to be familiar with the financial side of the marketing decisions, in order to have their decisions more and more rewarding. On this background the presiding theme of this book is to introduce certain concepts, tools and techniques of financial management and accounting procedures that are relevant to marketing functions.

The book is so designed that chapter one and two provides an insight in to the basis to marketing functions, chapters three to four focus attention on introducing basic financial and accounting inputs that are need full to the practing marketing professionals and the beginners. The approach of this book serves as an introduction to under stand the functional inter relationship between marketing and finance and that in turn help to have more productive utilization of resources at the disposal of marketers. Hope fully it is believed that the book will help in this process.

In preparing this book I have drawn help from marketing professionals and authors of related works, who have allowed me to make use of their expertise knowledge. I record my sincere thanks to them.

H. Peeru Mohamed

Contents

	Preface	v
1.	Marketing : The Conceptual Framework	1
2.	Marketing Mix	14
3.	Finance for Marketing	44
4.	Marketing Cost Analysis	84
5.	Marketing Cost Control : Techniques and Tools	107
6.	Accounting for Marketing Personnel	140
	Bibliography	173
	Index	175

I

Marketing : The Conceptual Framework

The Evolution

Marketing has emerged as a powerful system, in view of the growing challenges, the market offers. The consumers and Industrial Market today witness conditions such as huge market entry of a variety of new brands leading to heavy competition, continuous upgradation of technology leading to product differentiations, communication explosion leading to greater market awareness, increase in the measures so as to safeguard the consumers rights and so on. On these account the job of marketing has become risky, complex and challenge oriented assuming greater significance.

The significance gained by marketing is gradual. Under conditions of consumption oriented economy the concentration was only on consumption and no other economic activity was given due importance. The wants of people was then confined to the available products. This condition was followed by production oriented economy. Under production oriented economy people started production in accordance to their specific needs. The production oriented economy has four phases viz., production for self consumption, production for self consumption and exchange in terms of needful products, production for exchange alone. Production for exchange of products for money value has later resulted into production for the purpose of sales thus the sales oriented economy has emerged.

The sales concept which is dominant under sales oriented economy focus attention on the production of products at the first stage and by means of effective selling and promotion measures sales is effected that leads to earning of profit. The producer produces what he is capable of producing and he persuades the prospective buyer to purchase the same. It is based on the assumption that the prospective buyer will not buy normally unless he is compelled and insisted. The sales concept as narrated by Philip Kotler goes as below :

Starting point		Focus		Means		Ends
Factory	→	Product	→	Selling Promotion	→	Profits through Sales volume

The sales concept is applicable to conditions where the market has unlimited wants but limited supply of means to satisfy those wants and the producer without minding to understand the specific wants of the prospective buyer, produces the product.

In view of changing market scenario the sales concept based approach has become inefficient means to approach the prospective buyer. Under the changed market conditions the volume of production, the type of products, the number of brands in each product have immensely increased. The buyer is also left with considerably increased purchasing power and other means to purchase the products. Communication explosion has lead to higher level of awareness of product and market related issues. Thus the tactics adopted based on sales concept would not be sufficient enough to persuade the prospective buyer to make him purchase. In this context the need for marketing concept has emerged. The marketing concept, as Philip Kotler writes focus on "the key to achieve the organizational wants of target markets and deliver the desired satisfaction more effectively and efficiently than the competitions".

Theodore Levitt presents the distinction between the sales concept and marketing concept as "selling focus on the needs of the seller, marketing on the needs of buyer". Selling is preoccupied with sellers need to convert his product into cash, marketing with the idea of satisfying the needs of the customer by means of the product and the whole cluster of things associated with creating, delivering and finally consuming it.

The Concept

The concept of marketing as narrated by Philip Kotler runs as below :

Starting point	Focus	Means	Ends
Market →	Customer needs →	Coordinated marketing efforts →	Profit through consumer satisfaction

As could be seen from the above, the marketing concept gives importance to the consumer needs and by means of coordinated marketing efforts, the customer satisfaction is derived, which forms as the basis for the consumer satisfaction. The distinction between the sales concept and marketing concept is summarised in the following lines.

* Under sales concept the focus is on the product produced rather than on the consumer needs whereas under marketing concept the focus is on consumer needs.
* Under the sales concept the emphasis is on the corporate objectives and needs rather than the consumers need which is focused under the marketing concept.
* Priority is given to sales structure and thereby profit maximisation under sales concept whereas priority is given to consumer satisfaction and thereby profit maximisation under marketing concept.

The difference between the marketing and sales functions is much more than a semantic exercise. The difference can be summarised as below.

* Marketing is a wider activity and sales is one part of the wider activity.
* Sales activities are organised and exercised by the marketing department.
* Sales is concerned with transfer of goods from the producer to the prospective buyer. On the other hand marketing is concerned with customer satisfaction.

The gradual significance gained by marketing is presented in the following exhibits.

Significance Gained by Marketing

Exhibit I

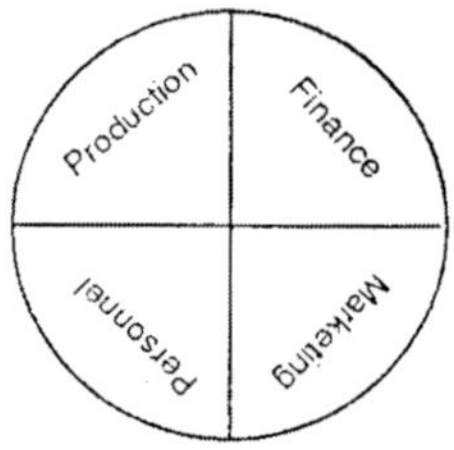

I Stage

Exhibit II

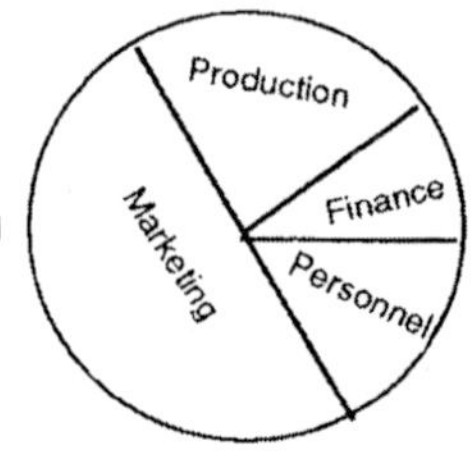

II Stage

Exhibit III

III Stage

Exhibit IV

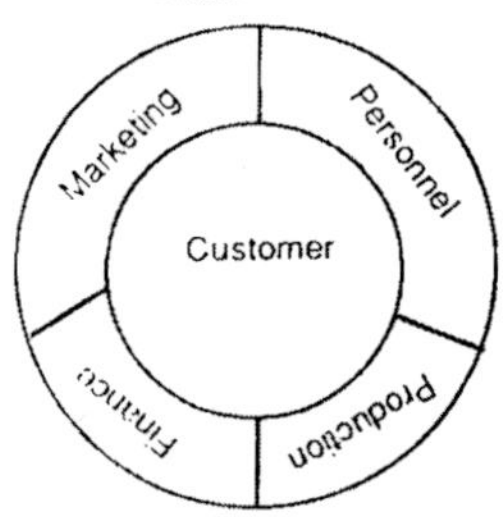

IV Stage

Exhibit V

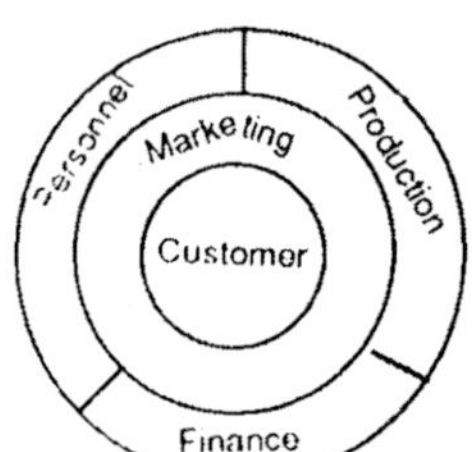

V Stage

Under exhibit I marketing is considered as a function similar to any other organisational function. However marketing gains greater significance and that is portrayed under Exhibit II. Marketing has gain still more significance and other managerial functions started revolving around marketing function and the situation is shown in Exhibit III. Exhibit IV presents customer as the focal point of marketing functions and other managerial functions being revolved in accordance to marketing. Exhibit V signifies that customer is the focal point and to satisfy them marketing acts as integrating which factor around all other functions like personnel, finance and production.

In the light of the above discussion marketing can be understood as a process involved in customer satisfaction. In order that customer satisfaction to be effectively achieved, identification of customers need become imperative. Thus marketing is a process of customers need identification, need fulfilment and satisfaction and thereby earning profit.

Marketing has been defined by Philip Kotler as "Marketing is a social and managerial process by which individuals and groups obtain what they need and want through creating offering and exchanging products of value with other". According to William F. Schoell "Marketing is a want satisfying social process". In the words of William J. Stanton "Marketing is a total system of interacting business activities designed to plan, price, promote and distribute satisfying products and services to present and potential customers".

In the light of the above definitions the author presents the definition to marketing as below

"Marketing is a total system based on the identified as well as identifiable needs of the prospective buyers and aim to satisfy those needs by offering appropriate means in such a way that the benefits received in the process is mutual for the buyer as well as the marketer".

From the definitions above it is obvious that marketing is customer oriented keeping their needs as the focal points.

Marketing Environment

Marketing environment refers to the environmental conditions under which marketing functions are to be performed. There is close linkage between marketing functions and the environment in which the organisation performing marketing functions are operating. The marketing environment can be classified under two broad heads viz., internal environment and external environment.

Internal environment relates to the internal conditions that exist within an organisation and such an environment is to a greater extent predictable, controllable, and adjustable. Generally the internal environment is concerned with the resources available to achieve the marketing goal such resources include man power, material, machinery, money, methods of production, managerial approach and the like. These resources should be considered in determining marketing goal and the strategy to achieve the same. Marketing functions cannot be performed effectively in isolation. Greater extent of coordination from production, personnel, financial and the related specialised functions is a must for effective operation of marketing functions. The functions such as production, finance, personnel are the base for the internal environment that shape the marketing activity.

External environment relates to the external conditions within which the market has to operate. The external conditions include political, social, cultural, geographical, ethical, technological, climatical and the demographics of consumers. Added to this the growing consumerism and the related aspects also form part of external environment.

The exhibits VI and VII present the environmental influences of marketing functions.

Marketer is supposed to be an environmentalist as he has to take into consideration of the changing external and internal environmental conditions which dominantly affects the marketing decision making.

Marketing Functions

The process of marketing essentially includes performance of a number of functions. Marketing functions are such of those marketing activities centered around achieving the marketing goals. Marketing functions are classified into many ways. Selected classifications are presented below.

According to Pyle marketing functions are divided as function of concentration and function of dispersion. The concentration and dispersion functions are further classified as shown below :

Exhibit VI: Environmental Influences on Marketing Functions

Exhibit: VII

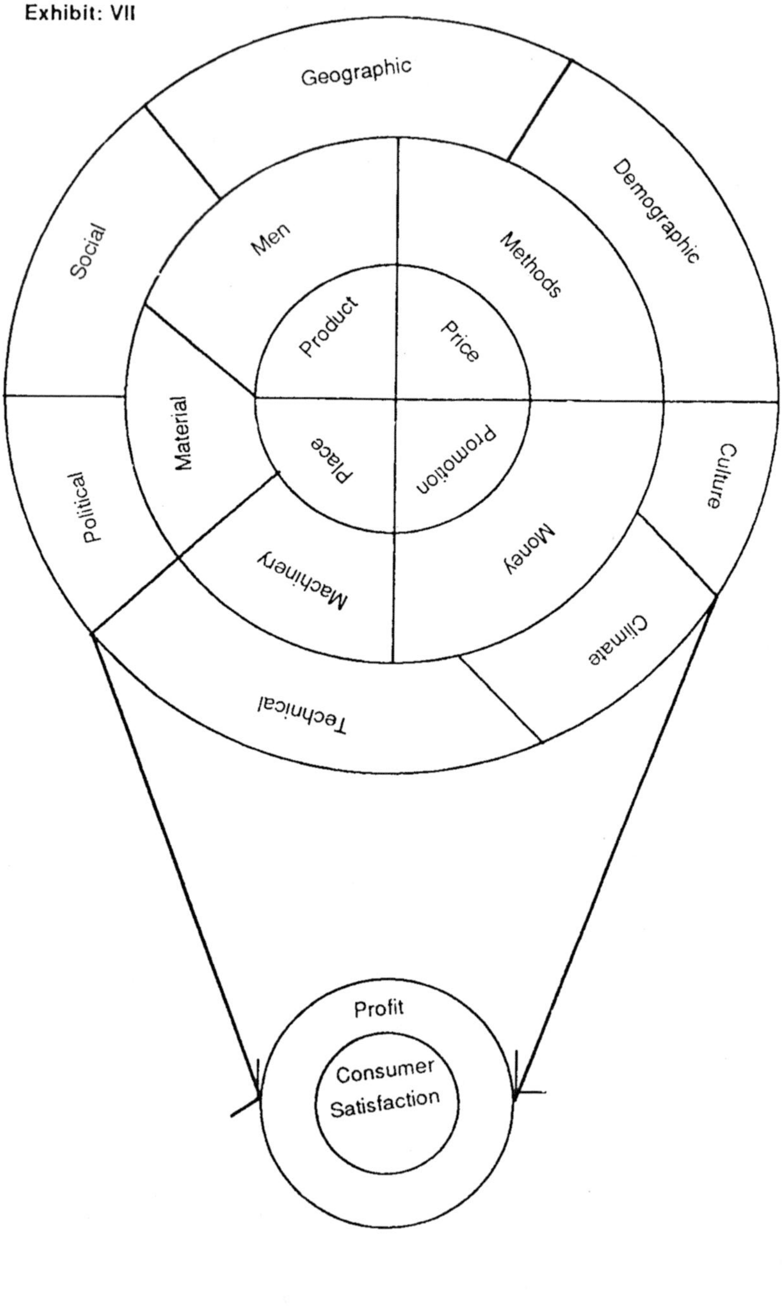
Geographic
Demographic
Culture
Climate
Technical
Political
Social
Men
Methods
Money
Machinery
Material
Product
Price
Promotion
Place
Profit
Consumer Satisfaction

Marketing Functions

Concentration	Dispersion
1. Buying or assembling	1. Selling
2. Transporting	2. Transporting
3. Storing	3. Storing
4. Grading	4. Grading
5. Financing	5. Financing
6. Risk bearing	6. Dividing

While the concentration function focus attention on the activities associated with buying or manufacturing, the dispersion function is related to distribution of the products in the target market.

From the economic point of view of Huegy and Mitchell classified functions as to functions creating time utility, place utility and possession utility. The classification is shown below,

Marketing Function

Creating Time and Place Utility	Creating Possession Utility
1. Transportation	1. Determining needs (gathering information)
2. Storing	2. Creating demand
3. Packing	3. Finding buyers and sellers
4. Dividing	4. Negotiating (Price and term)
5. Grading (Inspection/Sorting)	5. Giving advice (Adjusting goods and services to the needs of buyers).

Clark and Clark classifies the functions in the following way.

Marketing functions

Functions of Exchange	Function of Physical supply	Facilitating function
a. Selling	a. Transportation	a. Financing
b. Assembling and buying	b. Storage	b. Risk bearing
		c. Market information
		d. Standardisation

A review of the above ways of classification of functions enable to precisely present the function of marketing organisations in the following manner.

Marketing Function

Market Exploration	Market Entry	Market Expansion
a. Scanning environment	a. Market segmentation	a. Marketing Information system
b. Need identification	b. Branding and packaging	b. Market research
c. Product planning and development	c. Pricing	c. Marketing audit
d. Concept testing	d. Promotion	d. Public relation
	e. Launching	
	f. Distribution	

Market exploration is a function associated with exploring the market opportunity for a new product in an existing market or for an existing product in a new market. Exploration is the basic function which is to be performed consistently. The exploration function has been further grouped into four heads namely scanning the marketing environment, need identification and product planning and development and concept testing.

Scanning the market environment require analyzing both the internal and external environment (details has been dealt separately) and finding out the market opportunity followed by product planning and development in tune with the market opportunity. The product planning and development is a matching process, matching the market opportunity to the resource potentials available and thereby producing a product which is marketable. This will be followed by concept testing where the marketer will gain knowledge about the reaction to the product likely to be offered.

The second group of specific functions focus attention mainly on entry in the explored market. For this purpose the sub functions mainly to be performed are : pricing, branding, packaging, storage and physical distribution.

The final group of specific functions are concerned with market expansion which involves expanding the market share. Expansion requires understanding the existing position for which purpose marketing research, marketing audit and the like sub functions are to be performed.

Marketing : Need for Financial Approach

The efficiency of any organisation ultimately rests upon the mutual interdependence and interrelationship among various functional divisions of the organisation concerned. In this context the role of each division is significant. However the role of marketing is much more significant in view of the dynamically changing environmental conditions. Moreover the other functional divisions are organised in tune with the goals of the marketing divisions.

In a broader sense marketing is the act of administering the available internal resources from the viewpoint of prospective buyers. In view of the resource scarcity, making best use of limited resource is "sine qua non" in order to attain overall organizational efficiency.

Finance is one such scarce resource at the disposal of an organisation. Ultimately it is the financial availability that determine the extent of an activity, whatsoever may be its nature, and significance Marketing activity is therefore bound by the financial availability.

The process of marketing starts with identification of consumer needs and ends with fulfilment of the identified needs. This process involves a number of activities, the performance of which is based on financial availability. An insight into each activity will enable to understand the significance of financial approach.

The backbone of marketing activity is marketing research. Marketing research enables the formation of strategic marketing programme so as to reach the target market and thereby attain the marketing goals. The research activity involves collection of data, processing, analysing, interpreting and reporting. At each of these stages marketer has to make great amount of financial commitment. The available finance limits the extent of research activity.

Product mix of an organisation is a key decision area. The product mix consists of product lines and items appropriate to the needs of the target market segment. A product item may fetch return which is more than the normal market rate of return or less than that. In the matter of inclusion, retaining or deletion of a product line, or item the decision is bound by financial considerations.

Distribution network is the core functional area of marketing that connect the prospective buyer and the marketer. The choice of the distribution network is influenced by financial consideration. It is ultimately the financial affordability in terms of commission, brokerage, share of profit, and the like which influence the pattern of distribution as to intensive, extensive or selective.

The promotion tools usually comprises of advertisement, publicity, personal selling, sales promotion measures and other promotional measures. The choice of the components of the promotion mix, the communication media and the related aspects are also bound by financial consideration. In addition to the above components of promotion mix the activities like packaging, public relation etc also subject to financial availability.

The foregone components of marketing mix viz., product, distribution and promotion constitute the sources leading to outflow of finance. On the other hand the remaining constituent of the marketing mix viz., the price—the monetary value assigned to the product is a source that lead to inflow of finance. Price decisions assumes significant financial consideration. The pricing strategy may fall into two broad categories. Fixing higher margin leading to sale of lower units and lower margin leading to the sale of higher units. Irrespective of the strategy care should be devoted for the maximum possible inflow of finance. In relation to this objective the other components of the marketing mix may be suitably designed.

In view of the financial perspective associated with the functional aspects of marketing as detailed above marketer in addition to his expertised knowledge in all aspects concerned with marketing of a product is also expected to acquire thorough knowledge in the financial aspects that are detrimental to the marketing decision making. Financial knowledge will enable to arrive at implement and to control marketing decisions more meaningfully and profitability. The vital areas wherein financial knowledge will be more useful to the marketer include :

* product mix decisions
* Product diversification
* Product positioning
* Determination of sales mix
* Determination of sales volume
* Promotion mix decision
* Budgets in relation to functional areas of marketing
* Price fixation
* Fixation of terms of sales
* Fixation of credit collection period
* Working capital management
* Inventory management
* Sales forecasting
* Cost volume profit analysis
* Capital investment decisions
* Marketing audit
* Market performance control measures
* Market related financial information and the like.

The knowledge gained by the marketer on the above as well as similar lines will enable him to make the decisions, financially viable and rational. In the light of these views a financial approach towards marketing management gains prominence.

2

Marketing Mix

Marketing mix refers to the offerings made by an organisation in order to satisfy their target buyers. The marketing mix consists of

..... Product
..... Place
..... Price
..... Promotion

The above four component of marketing mix are popularly known as 4 p's of marketing. These components are interrelated and any decision pertaining to one invariably affects the other three. A detailed discussion on each component of the marketing mix is presented below.

Product

Product is defined as "bundle of satisfaction". Anything that offer some amount of satisfaction is considered as product. A consumer who is left with an unfulfilled but identified need require a mean to satisfy that need and product serves as a mean to satisfy that need. Product plays significant role in the marketing program of any organisation and all other elements in the marketing mix are arranged in tune with the nature of the products only. Philip Kotler express product as "anything that can be offered to a market for attention, acquisition, use or consumption that might satisfy a want or need".

The products may take the following shape:

1 * Generic product 2 * Expected product
3 * Augmented product
4 * Potential product

The purpose of making a purchase is to attain an ultimate satisfaction from the product concerned. A buyer buying a watch is ultimately aiming for satisfaction with respect to time. This is otherwise called core benefit. The core benefit is converted into a generic product which refers to the basic minimum requirement to satisfy the core benefit desired by the buyer. In case of the watch just a mechanism to show an accurate time constitutes the generic product, expected product refers to a set of attributes and conditions that gives further benefits. Augmented product refers to additional functional attributes and conditions that give additional benefit to the buyer. In case of watch providing dates, alarm and the like functions make the product as the augmented product.

In view the competitive conditions the augmented product will undergo changes in tune with consumers expectation on the one hand and competitive offerings on the other hand. The product will incorporate all possible features and thus stand as a potential product. It is to be noted that in the under developed or developing nations the market will offer products which are at the level of expected product or augmented product. The potential product dominates the market of developed nations.

Product Mix

Product mix refers to such of those products which are offered to the market by a company. Product mix consist of different product lines and each product line consists of different product items.

Product line refers to those items of product meant to satisfy a specific set of wants of the consumer. Product items refer to the individual product in the line.

A company offers cosmetic items, office furniture, domestic furniture, office machines and equipment. All these things put together may be called as its product mix. The product mix may consist of different lines such as cosmetics line, office furniture line and so on. Each line consists of product items such as in the case of cosmetics where soap, shampoo, face creams etc. are offered.

The company offering product mix may have related product line or unrelated product line. The related line is one in which some mode of relationship between one line and the other line will be there. For example a company offering office furniture may offer office machines as the other line and so on. Unrelated product line refers to line which are not related to one another for example a company offering cosmetic line may also start publishing books and journals.

Adding or deletion of a product line or item assumes vital significance. Such a decision arise out of following influences

* The preference by prospective buyer
* The offerings by competitors
* Technological upgradation
* Profitability associated
* Resource utilisation
* Capacity utilisation
* By-product utilisation and so on.

Types of Products

The product may be classified on the following basis :

1. Based on Durability

a. Durable Goods : Durable goods are those which are available for repeated uses. Such goods without loosing their functional utility will survive for a longer period of time. The examples includes Television, Refrigerators etc.

b. Non-durable Goods : These are goods meant for limited or single use only. Example include soap, cold drink and so on.

2. On the Basis of Shopping Habits

(a) Convenience Goods : Convenience goods are those which the consumer regularly buy with minimum shopping efforts. Usually habits dominate the choice of the product and the price will be normally very low. The example includes cigarette, news paper and so on. Convenience goods may be further classified in to stable, impulse and emergency goods. This classification is based on the regularity and urgency associated with purchase.
(b) Shopping Goods : Shopping goods refers to those the consumer select after careful comparison of competitors brand. The

consumer will spend considerable amount of time in searching, evaluating information concerned with the goods to arrive at the ultimate decision. Shopping products may be classified into homogeneous and heterogeneous. Generally in the case of homogeneous products price is the only criteria for selecting a product and on the contrary heterogeneous products takes into account price as well as other attributes like brand image package and so on.

(c) Speciality Goods : Speciality products are those which have unique characteristics. Special purchase effort is to be put in for buying such products. The example include aesthetic products. Usually such products are highly priced.

3. On the Basis of User

(a) Consumer Goods : These are goods used by the ultimate consumer for the purpose of consumption. It may fall into any one of the categories explaind above.

(b) Industrial Products : These are goods used by industrial user for the purpose of further manufacturing, processing and so on. Raw materials, capital equipment, accessory items etc., fall in this category.

(c) Unsought Products : Unsought products are those products the existence of which the potential buyer is not aware of. As such the products in this category does not fall within the purview of the product selection.

4. On the Basis of Tangibility

On the basis of tangibility products may be classified as intangible and tangible. The classification discussed above falls under the tangible product category.

Intangible goods : Intangible goods refers mainly to the services offered for sales. Such service include, restaurant service, medical service, financial service and the like.

Product Positioning

In the context of multiple brands competing high each other in the market, product positioning assumes significance. Positioning generally refers to the way of determining and creating a desired achieving a place in the consumers perception, about the brand in relation to the competitors brand.

A firm may adopt-different positioning strategies depending on the market, consumer and the product characteristics.

Positioning involves creating a Perceptual mapping of a product by measuring the similarity and dissimilarity between the products which the consumer has in his mind already and deciding the way in which the firm is to position its products, the means to increase the preference level of the product and rating it higher than any other brand already being perceived by the consumer.

Product positioning involves a thorough analysis of the brand in terms of its functional utilities. Based on that the unique selling proposition will be selected and attempts will be made to make that unique selling proposition reach the prospective consumers mind. The product positioning strategy ultimately depend upon the specific requirement of the target market. Target market and position strategy are inseparable and mutually depended.

The position strategy involves the following :

* Brand attribute analysis
* Consumer segmentation
* Determination of target buyer
* Perceptual mapping
* Search for vacant positions

The brand attribute analysis find answer to question such as (1) What the product is ? (2) To whom it is meant for ? (3) What are the benefits the product can offer and the like ?

The consumer segmentation relates to division of consumers on desired basis and selecting the target group of buyers.

The technique of brand positioning depends:

Image Profile Analysis

It is one of the most widely used techniques. By this technique the consumers perception as regards competitive brands is measured. The profile analysis will present the strength and weakness of competitors brand and a meaningful observation will also yield the consumer expectation, based on which the position strategy will be shaped. Brand image profile for four detergent powder.

	1	2	3	4
Cleaning ability				
Colour protection				
Reasonable price				
Gentle on hands				
Easy solubility				
Brightening ability				
Remake of grime				
Foaming capacity				
Colour of detergent				

Factor Analysis

Under this method large number of variables pertaining to the product is collected. The correlation coefficients between all possible pairs of original variable is found. The factors which are uncorrelated are listed out. This enables identification of factors related to the brand. The most important factor so identified will pave the way for positioning.

In addition to these technique cluster analysis method, where the similarity as well as dissimilarity between the items in a cluster of brands are studied. Multi dimensional scaling method is also used for this purpose.

Example of certain leading position strategy in India

Product Brand	Position Strategy
Limca	Thirst quenching
Thumbs-up	Refreshment
Rasna	Economy
Oberoi Hotel	Luxury
Hero Honda	Economy
Vimal Sarees	Fashion
Surf	White
Maggi Noodle	Fast to cook

Right positioning enable easy marketing. A product cannot be everything to everyone but it is something to some one. That something is to be identified and rightly portrayed to make positioning very effective.

Product Life Cycle

Every product has to undergo a series of stages throughout its stay in the market. Such stages the product undergo is called as the life cycle of the product. The life cycle of the product usually consists of the following stages :

1. Introduction
2. Growth
3. Maturity
4. Saturation
5. Decline

Introduction

It is the stage at which the product is introduced in the market. The product assumes the status of a new product, waiting for the consumer acceptance. The sales will be normally very low due to lack of consumer awareness and acceptance. Usually the marketers has to put in serious launching efforts to position the product in the market.

Growth

The introduction stage will be followed by the growth stage. At this stage the product has started gaining the consumer acceptance and the sales volume started increasing. At this stage greater amount of sales promotion efforts are essential for effective marketing of the product concerned.

Maturity

At this stage the product reaches the maximum share in the market. The product would have gained loyal consumers. At the same time competitive products would have entered and they will pose challenge to this product. In order to maintain and to expand the market share the marketer has to go in for product modification, diversifiction and the like strategies.

Saturation

It is a stage in which there is neither increase nor decrease in the volume of sale. A thorough modification in the attribute of the product is needed to attract new consumers. Competitors products at this stage would have started gaining its market share.

Decline

Decline is a stage whereby the market share of the product will consistently go down. In the meantime the sales of competitors products market share will tend to withdraw the product from the market or to go in for complete modification. The above stage is illustrated here.

Product Planning and Development

In a competitive market situation the function product planning and development assumes greater significance. Product planning and development is concerned with mainly two aspects viz., (1) making significant changes in the existing product. (2) introducing a new product.

Making significant changes in the existing product is a continuous process of any effective marketing strategy in order to retain existing customers and attract the new customers. Such significant change may take place by incorporating modifications in any one or more of the attributes associated with the product viz., package, colour, size, content, quality, price, functional utility and so on. The purpose of such continuous change is to make the product more competitive by adopting the technical advancements and also to provide satisfaction to consumer taking into account of the changing requirements.

New Product Development

New product development is associated with creation of products which are new to the target market concerned. Such new product may be absolutely new product or relatively new product. An absolutely new product is one which is of the first of its kind whereas a relatively new product is that which comes out with significant changes in the product already offered. Absolute new product arise of constant research and development under technologically advanced condition. Hence absolutely new products are common phenomena under developed nations only. On contrary developing countries are concerned with "creative imitation" whereby already introduced products under some other market condition will be imitated after administering creativity, suitably and introduced in the market.

The new product development has to undergo the following stages :

1. Searching
2. Screening
3. Business analysis
4. Test marketing
5. Commercialisation

Searching is a stage whereby idea for new product is constantly searched. In developed nation agencies such as product venture team consisting of technically and professionally qualified personnel will include themselves in search for idea usually the research and development wing of the organisation will be left with the job of searching new ideas. An ideal marketing manager's responsibility area include new idea generation also. In addition to this competitors, consumers, middlemen will also be helpful in providing idea for new product development.

All the idea searched and gathered are to be screened on the basis of selected criteria. Screening therefore is a process of analyzing, deleting and selecting suitable ideas. Suitable as to organizational goals, marketing goals, the market conditions, buyers choice, technical feasibility and so on.

Screening will be followed by business analysis stage in which the ideas are scanned through from the business point of view i.e., cost benefit analysis, profitability, marketability, technical feasibility, competing ability and so on. On satisfactory results the business analysis and product concept is developed and will be subjected to test marketing.

Test marketing is a process whereby the product produced on sample basis will be introduced and tested among selected segments of the market as to its acceptability by the target buyers. It is a very important stage in the sense that further attempts on marketing of the product rest upon the outcome of the test market. The outcome of test market and the sequence to be followed is exhibited below :

The introduction or modification or deletion as explained, depends upon the outcome of to test marketing as to good, fair or poor.

In order to gain the factual picture, process of test marketing should be performed rationally and scientifically without any bias. The segment of market should be appropriate representative of the overall market otherwise the marketing will present misleading results.

The commercialisation is the final stage depending on the outcome of test marketing. A good or fair outcome of test marketing will lead to launching the product in the target market and thus the commercialisation begins.

Place (Distribution)

Distribution refers to the activities involved in the movement of the goods from the production center to the consumption center. It includes not only the physical activities such as transporting, storage etc. but also the activities involved in the transfer of ownership of the product. Distribution channel is defined by cundiff et al as "the path traced in the direct or indirect transfer of ownership of a product as it moves from the producer to the ultimate consumer or industrial user".

The conventional distribution channel for consumer goods may be of the following types.

1. Producer → consumer
2. Producer → wholesale/retailer → consumer
3. Producer → wholesales → retailer → consumer
4. Producer → agents → wholesaler → retailer → consumer

Under level 1 : the producer directly distributing the products to the consumer without the involvement of any middlemen. This method is called zero level distribution. Under level, 2 : there exist a single middlemen who may be either wholesaler or retailer who get the goods from the producer and transfer it to the consumer concerned. Under level, 3 : which is the most common pattern of distribution, the goods are moving from the producer to the wholesaler and from the wholesaler to retailer and finally from retailer to the ultimate consumer.

Conventional channel has the characteristics that the middlemen are bound by agreements and the consideration for the agreement is the commission. The effective distribution depends upon the effective performance of the distribution operation by each middlemen in the distribution channel. Under this condition ineffective performance by even one set of middlemen will affect the whole distribution system adversely.

The vertical distribution pattern practiced in some countries takes the following shape. In the vertical pattern producer, wholesaler and retailer join together and they are the co-owners who are bound by the consideration of sharing the profit. They perform their role in the distribution function in view of their specialised talents.

The Channel Choice

The choice of distribution channel is a crucial decision and the following factors influence the channel decision :

* Middlemen
* Product
* Consumer
* Market location
* Geographical spread of consumers
* Man power available
* Competitors channel pattern
* Infrastructural facilities available
* Marketing strategy followed
* Communication network available

The Intensity of Distribution

The intensity of distribution is the channel plan associated with the extent of distribution operation. There are three degrees of intensity viz.,

1. Intensive distribution
2. Selective distribution
3. Exclusive distribution

The intensive distribution aims at maximum exposure of the product to the target buyers. The products which are subject to intensive distribution are convenience products like cigarettes, chewing gums, soft drinks and the like. The underlying fact is that the prospective buyers will be tempted to make the purchase of those items which are being exposed to them.

Selective distribution is done on basis of careful selection of sales point, sales persons who are compatible with the products image. Usually shopping products and industrial products are being distributed selectively.

Exclusive distribution is further step in selective distribution. It is mostly suitable for speciality products with unique distinctiveness. Mostly producers will deal in exclusive distribution directly without involving middlemen by opening exclusive sales points.

Wholesale Distribution

Wholesale distribution refers to distribution of products from the production center to the retailers. According to Cundiff and Still "Wholesalers buy and sell merchandise to the retailers and other merchants and not to the consumers". The American Marketing Association defines wholesalers as "wholesalers buy and resell merchandise to retailers and other merchants and to industrial institutions and commercial users but do not sell in significant amount to ultimate consumers".

Types of Wholesalers

The wholesalers may be classified under several heads.

(a) On the basis of area of operation

- i. Local wholesalers
- ii. District or state wholesalers
- iii. National wholesalers

(b) On the basis of product line

- i. General merchandise wholesaler
- ii. General line wholesalers
- iii. Speciality wholesalers

(c) On the basis of method of operation

- i. Full service wholesaler
- ii. Limited function wholesaler

Services of Wholesalers

The wholesalers renders enormous service to the producers as well as to the retailers.

Services to Producers

Services to producers include the following :

* Financial assistance
* Market information
* Storage facilities
* Promotional help
* Sharing risk
* Market expansion
* Managing salesforce
* Enhance utility to the product
* Price maintenance
* Transportation

Services to Retailers

The services to retailers include the following :

* Supply of goods in time
* Sales promotion
* Storage and warehousing
* Transportation
* Credit facilities
* Market information

Retail Distribution

Retail distribution has been defined by American Marketing Association as "Retailing consists of activities involved in selling directly to the ultimate consumer for personal non business use." According to Cundiff et. al. "Retailer is a merchant or occasionally an agent whose main business is selling directly to the ultimate consumer".

Classification of Retailers

Retailers may be classified under two broad heads :

(1) Small Scale Retailers

Small scale retailers are those who assume the following characteristics

* Limited capacity investment
* Limited line of business

* Sole trader form of organisation
* Flexible operation
* Mostly seasonal business
* Limited consumers and so on

The small scale retailers include hawkers, peddlers, cheapjacks, market traders, street vendors, petty shop keepers, street stall holders, second hand goods dealers, general shop keepers and the like.

2. Large Scale Retailers

Large scale retailers assumes the following characteristics :

* High capital investment
* Wider line of business
* Company or partnership form of business operation
* Fixed base of business
* Large number of consumers and so on.

The large scale retailers include departmental stores, chain stores, mail order business houses, hire purchases and instalment sales, co-operative societies, super markets, shopping complexes and the like.

Services of Retailers

By virtue of their position, the retailers render commendable services to the wholesalers and the consumers such services include :

* Sale at small lot
* Credit facilities
* Selling at the doorsteps
* After sales services
* Providing additional utility to the product
* Sharing risks
* Provide variety of goods
* Provide product information
* Supply according to requirements

Promotion

Promotion refers to the efforts put forth by marketer to induce the prospective buyer to get in favour of the Products Marketed.

Promotion mix of a marketer consists of the following submixes viz.,

1. Advertising
2. Sales promotion
3. Personal selling
4. Publicity
5. Public relation and
6. Packaging

Advertising

Advertising has been defined by Schoell as "Any paid form of non personal communication through mass media about a product or idea by an identified sponsor". Advertising as a component of the promotion mix assumes the following distinctive qualities as explained by Philip Kotter.

Public Presentation

Advertising is communication to the public at large.

Pervasiveness

The seller is permitted to repeat the message as much as he likes. The buyer is also in a position to receive and compare the message from the competitors.

Amplified Expressiveness

Utilising the artful print, sound and colour etc, the company's products are expressed in such a way that the target buyer's attention is gained.

Impersonal

Advertising as it is impersonal cannot compel anyone to be attentive towards the advertisements. It is a monologue with target audience.

Objectives of Advertising

The objectives with which advertising is done by any marketer is generally falls into any one or more of the following :

* To announce changes
* To create awareness
* To remind the consumer
* To launch a product
* To expand the market
* To communicate
* To explain the product features, utility etc.
* To persuade the consumers.

Media of Advertising

Media refers to the tool through which the advertising messages are conveyed in the target Market. The usual media available are :

* Print
* Broadcast
* Telecast, video
* Mailing
* Film
* Posters
* Leaflets
* House journal
* Display signs.

Each one of the above media has its own merit as well as demerits. The choice of a media for the purpose of advertising is Influenced by the considerations such as :

* Product
* Buyer
* Competitors
* Market
* Availability of media
* Resource
* Life cycle of the product
* Market share and the like.

Advertising Decision

The advertising decision of a marketer involves the following decisions.

The Advertisement Techniques

The advertisement technique of any organisation aims to achieve multiple objectives. In order that the advertisement objectives are to be attained the advertisement message are to be suitably arranged to draw the attention, to develop interest and desire and ultimately act on the desired direction. The following are some of the advertisement concepts popularly adopted.

Celebrity

In this type of advertisement celebrities are selected and used to introduce convince, to remind the products. Celebrities in view of their credibility are able to easily create convictions in the mind of the prospective buyers, usually sports persons, singers, film stars are used as celebrities.

Case History

In this type the messages are conveyed narrating the usage of the products and the experience thereby projecting a real life situation to adopt the product advertised.

Demonstration

The products in this method are being demonstrated with respect to its various functional utilities.

Humorous

The messages are conveyed in a humorous way that will keep the target buyer in a lighter mood and thereby their attention is drawn.

Sex Appeal

Administering sex appeal to draw the attention of the target audience is very often practiced, irrespective of the relevance of the products

Children

Usage of children as ad model has been on the increase. The products and their usage utility is projected from the children's viewpoint so as to reach the mind of their parents through their children.

Musical Effect

Concentration of musical effect of advertisement is on the increase. It is based on the fact that anything conveyed musically will be well received as music is considered as the common language of human being of the universe.

Technical Expertise

This involves the usage of technical expertise in photography, colour sequences and presentation.

The above are popular techniques of ads being practiced.

The Requirements of Good Advertisement

Good advertisement require to have certain values such as sentimental value, cultural value, ethical value, social value, educational value, entertainment value, informational value and so on.

Advertisement should be so designed to confirm to the regulation of country and should not offend against the morality, decency and religious susceptibilities of the people. The general rules of conduct with respect to Indian advertisement is specified in the report of working group on autonomy for Akashvani and Doordarshan, Ministry of Information and Broadcasting, Government of India. Some important general rules are listed below.

No advertisement should be permitted

1. Which discretes any race, caste, colour creed nationality except where in such usage would be for specific purpose of effective dramatization such as combating prejudice.
2. Which is against any objectives, principles or provision of the Constitution of India.

3. Which will tend to incite people to crime or promote disorder, violence or breach of law or which presents criminality as desirable or furnish details of crime of imitation thereof.
4. Which would adversely affect the friendly relation with foreign states.
5. Which would adversely offer the friendly relation with foreign states.
6. Which exploits national emblem or any part of the constitution or national leader or state dignitary.
7. Advertisement must not be directed towards religious or political end.
8. Advertisements concerned with television, the following are not acceptable.

   a. Cigarettes and tobacco products
   b. Money lenders
   c. Chit funds

Saving scheme other than conducted by nationalised banks or recognised financial institutions.

   d. Matrimonial agencies
   e. Unlicensed employment agencies
   f. Fortune tellers and those with the claim of hypnotism
   g. Betting/Guide books related to horse race.
   h. Advertising should not contain disparaging reference to another product or service.
   i. All other respects the Director General All India Radio/ Doordarshan be referred for purpose of commercial broadcasting and telecasting on All India Radio/ Doordarshan for code of ethics issued by the Advertising Council of India as modified from time to time.
   j. Notwithstanding anything contained herein this code is subject to such modification, direction as may be made or issued by Government of India from time to time.

Sales Promotion

Sales promotion methods are techniques used to induce directly or indirectly the middlemen or the ultimate user towards making the final choice of the product.

The types of sales promotion differs in accordance with the product, consumer, market and resource, and the environmental considerations. Also there is no general agreement on the sales promotion techniques. Under certain circumstances what one classify as personal selling or publicity may be considered as sales promotion techniques under different circumstances.

The popular sales promotion techniques with their relative features are listed below :

	Technique		Feature
	Coupons	-	Induce trail purchase
		-	Reach large number of customers
		-	Not suitable for unfamiliar products
2.	Contents and sweep stakes	-	Create excitement targeted to group of consumers
		-	Require heavy media
3.	Bonus package	-	Increase frequency of purchase
		-	Develop habit of demanding bonus items
		-	Better retail technique
4.	Price-offs	-	Flexible
		-	Controllable
		-	Seasonal
		-	Not helpful loyalists
5.	Free in Mail	-	Effective retail
		-	Attract new customers
		-	Extensive advertising
		-	Need effective method of handling offer
		-	Further effective method of handling offer
		-	Further purchase is doubtful.
6.	Refunds	-	Effective to boost the sales
		-	Can be targeted to limited group only.
7.	Trade coupons	-	Effective in making trial purchase, include trade cooperation.

8. Trade allowance	- Flexible
	- Requires less time
	- Will not pass from retailer to consumer
9. Samples	- Selective
	- Attractive
	- Make trial purchase
	- Expensive
10. Point of purchase materials	- Very effective advertising impact
	- Make trial purchase
	- Display effect
	- Loss expensive
11. Trade shows	- Effective
	- Demonstrative effect
	- Better communication
12. Gift/Free merchandise	- Effective
	- Induce trail purchase
	- Attract channel members
13. Tie-in-promotion	- Two or more brands teamed up by coupons refunds contests etc.
14. Patronage awards	- Values in cash according to patronage improve sales volume

The sales promotion measures aims to generate immediate purchase. They are focused on three groups namely consumers (called as consumer promotion) middlemen (called as trade promotion) and sales force (called as sales force promotion).

As on date the importance of sales promotion is on the increase in view of the immediate and direct benefit marketer receives, compared to administrating any other promotion technique.

Personal Selling

Personal selling refers to the face to face marketing communication with the prospective buyer based on the ultimate intention to induce him to act favourably towards the purchase of a product. Personal selling as a promotion technique has increasingly gained the acceptance in view of the merits associated therewith. The personal selling involves mainly the following components i.e.,

* Sales presentation
* Sales meetings and
* Telemarketing

Under sales presentation and sales meeting the sales force appointed by marketer directly involves themselves in personal compensation and evoke on the spot response from the target buyer. On the other hand under tele marketing the sales personnel contact prospective buyers over telephone and conveys the sales message to convince them towards the desired action.

All the three components listed above involves effective sales personnels. The sales personnel may be of the following types :

1. Deliver : Such sales personnel are concerned with mere delivery of the products only (e.g. : News papers, milk etc.)
2. Order taker : Such sales personnel are concerned with receiving orders for goods from the buyer. (e.g. : In a restaurant the person receiving orders for the eatables)
3. Missionary : Those who spread the knowledge about the product and creating buyer/seller relationship (e.g. : a medical representative)
4. Technician : Concerned with technical aspects of the products. On request from the user of the product he will attend the user and rectify problem if any.
5. Demand creator : Those who insist, induce, convince and motivate the prospective buyer to act in favour of purchase of a product.

The Selling Process

The selling process by sales personnel has the following stages :

1. Prospecting and qualifying
2. Pre approach

3. Approach
4. Presentation and demonstration
5. Handling objection
6. Follow up

Prospecting and qualifying refers to identification of the prospective buyer. This is done by means of referring to the company's past records, contacting present customers referring telephone directories canvassing to any one by taking a chance and so on. This will be followed by pre approach where in the nature, specific need, prospective buyers characteristics are gathered and analysed which will enable the next stage namely approach. In the approach stage the prospective buyer will be contacted in person and the sales person acquaint himself with the prospective buyer afterwards the presentation and demonstration stage commences, in which the product is suitably explained in relation to its functional utilities. In the process the doubts, objections raised by the prospective buyer are to be carefully handled and cleared to the best satisfaction of the prospective buyer and assumes the next stage. The next stage 'closing' is associated with completion of the sales talk by inducing the prospective buyer to place order. At this stage the sales person may come at with special discounts or free gifts and the like so as to induce the prospect to place order. The 'final stage' is the follow up wherein a schedule of follow-up actions for repeated purchase and related activities are to be planned.

Qualities of Sales Personnel

In order to come out effectively in the selling process the sales personnels are to necessarily have the following qualities, as identified by a marketing research group of United States of America.

1. Acceptance of responsibility
2. Aggressiveness
3. Appreciation of importance of selling
4. Care of health (Physical, mental and financial)
5. Courtesy
6. Dependability
7. Determination

8. Friendliness
9. Industriousness
10. Initiative
11. Integrity
12. Judgment
13. Knowledge of the product
14. Persuasiveness
15. Resourcefulness
16. Sales ethics
17. Self management
18. Sincerity
19. Understanding of buying motives
20. Work organisation

Administration of Sales Personnel

The administration of sales personnel essentially involve the following main functions.

* Recruitment
* Training
* Compensation
* Control

Recruitment

Recruitment of sales persons involves the following steps.

1. Job analysis and description
2. Fixation of specific requirement
3. Selection of source of recruitment
4. Inviting applications
5. Screening applications
6. Testing
7. Interviewing
8. Preliminary selection
9. Final selection

The job analysis and description is concerned with the nature of job to be performed by the sales personnel. Usually the job of a sales person consists of three categories :

i. Making the sales
  To book orders
  To get orders repeated
  To make promotion efforts
ii. Servicing
  To provide advise and assistance
  To enable selection
  To attend after sales requirements
iii. Administration
  To maintain sales records
  To plan sales meetings
  To report on sales trend

As per the nature of job the specific qualification to perform the job will be fixed. The selection sources will then be contacted. The sources include, colleges, private employment agencies, and the like. On receipt of the application the screening is to be performed so as to restrict to the applicants who are most suited. The screened applicants will be tested. The test consists of ability test, habitual characteristic test, achievement test and so on.

Such of those who have performed satisfactorily in the tests in accordance with the norms laid down they will be interviewed and preliminary selection will be done. Subject to medical examination and other requirements as per the regulation of the organisation concerned the final selection will be made.

Training

Training assumes significance. The selected personnels are to be offered proper training so that they will perform their functions effectively. Training facilitate acquiring knowledge and skill essential to perform the job offered. The training programme fall in to any of these method of a blend of all of these methods.

* Lecture method
* Audio visual method
* Discussion method
* Conference method
* Role playing method
* Panel method
* Brain storming
* On the job method

Compensation

Compensation is concerned with the remuneration payable to the sales personnel. Appropriate compensation method is a must to make the sales person to contribute significantly in his job. The usual methods of compensation are :

1. Straight or fixed salary
2. Straight commission
3. Combined payment of salary and commission
4. Combined payment of salary, commission and bonus
5. Reimbursements of expenses, commission and bonus

Control

In order to ensure the desired direction of the performance of any activity and to make corrective action, the control is a must. Control consists of verifying as to whether everything occurs in conformity with the proposed plans. The sales personnel will be controlled by means of personal contact as also through reports records etc. Control by means of personal contact involves field supervision and surprise visits by higher officials. Reports and records generlly reveal the following :

1. Number of calls made
2. Amount of sales volume
3. Amount of sales lost
4. The reasons behind increase/demand in the sales
5. Extent of competition
6. Complaints attended

Based on the above records the performance of the sales persons can be controlled and motivated properly towards better performance.

Publicity

Publicity constitutes as another method of sales promotion. Philip Kotter defines publicity as "Securing editorial space as divorced from paid space in all media, read, viewed or heard by a company's customers or prospects for the specific purpose of assisting in meeting the sales goals.

Publicity is considered as a more dependable tool of promotion in the sense that the potentials of the product concerned is been conveyed by external agencies who gain no benefit over the sale of such product being promoted. Those prospects who otherwise avoid advertisement or sales person may yield to publicity. Editorial write-ups, lobbying, counselling etc are forming part of publicity measures.

Public Relation

Publicity and public relation are sometimes viewed as one and the same. However both are different. Public relation is a function organised scheduled and executed by the firm in order to maintain and improve cardinal relationship with public so as to achieve the marketing goal. Publicity on the other hand originate from agencies, media and the like who are other than the firm concerned. Market oriented public relation is gaining importance in view of its multiple advantages. The marketing oriented public relation activities centered around the following aspects.

* Creating cardinal atmosphere between the society and the marketer.
* Creating mental awareness and understanding
* Bringing together the marketer and the society by effective approaches.

The major techniques used in maintaining public relation include.

* Publications
* Sponsoring events
* Engaging public utility activities
* Involvement in charitable programme
* Participation in societal problems.

Packaging

Packaging is concerned with finding a wrapper or cover suitable to the product. Package eventhough more a production related function in view of the additional functions it renders viz to attract and induce the prospective buyers, packaging is considered more as a promotion tool than merely or wrapper, or a cover along with the product.

The major functions of package are to enable

1. Protection of product
2. Preservation of product
3. Positioning the product and
4. Promoting the product

The packaging witnesses a changing scenario, as a result of technological improvement in the packaging materials and packaging techniques. Package has gained increased attention from the manufacturers and is practiced widely. There has been manifold increase in quality, appearance, usage, utility of the package. The consumer market today witnesses refill, reuse and multi purpose packages. Package has been suitably termed as silent salesman.

Price

Pricing decisions are very important in the sense that the sales revenue ultimately depends on the price policy of the organisation concerned. The price charged for a product should be appropriate taking into account, the following considerations viz.,

1. Cost of production
2. Competitive environment
3. Consumer attitude
4. Product characteristics
5. Distribution channel
6. Government policy
7. Marketing strategy
8. Life cycle of the product
9. Pricing objectives.
10. Economic conditions

The pricing methods usually adopted are as follows :

1. Cost Plus Pricing Method

Under this method the total cost of the product will be estimated taking into account of the fixed cost as well as variable cost. The total cost will be added with desired percentage of the profit. The desired percentage of profit however depends upon the considerations explained above. This method of pricing is more simple and rational. This method is suitable when the product is in the perfect market conditions and the product is in its maturity or growth stage as the case it may be.

2. Marginal Cost Pricing

This method of price fixation takes into account only the variable cost and not the total cost. The variable cost plus desired percentage of profit will form the price for the product. This method is useful under highly competitive situation also when the product is at its introductory or decline or repositioning stage.

The choice of the method of pricing however depends upon the pricing objectives. The pricing objectives include the following:

1. To reach a target rate of return
2. To lead the market
3. To expand market share
4. To prevent competitors
5. To position the product
6. To stabilize product and the like.

Pricing for New Product

There are two specific methods in practice with regard to pricing for new product. They are

1. High Skimming Pricing Method

Under this method a high initial price will be charged with the objective of profit maximisation at the shortest possible time. This method will be practiced income of products which has short period market and also subject to heavy competition. Therefore the marketer want to maximise the profit when the distinctiveness is unique, while high price create a vision of superior product it goes with the disadvantage of difficulty in introducing the product as the price is abnormally high.

2. Low Penetration Method

Under this method a low price will be charged and once there is market acceptance for the product the price will then be increased gradually. It is a reverse method to the high swimming pricing policy method. In view of the lower price introduction of the product is easy.

In addition to the above the market witness pricing methods such as—

Psychological pricing : Depends on the psychology of the target buyer prices may be fixed higher or lower. In the target market price is considered as the yardstick to measure quality, accordingly the price will be fixed higher. Marketers, sometime uses 'Odd-Pricing' such as Rs.90.95 to give a psychological impression that the prices are exact and accurate.

Customary Pricing : Under this method prices are fixed based on the basis on the local custom's and expectations of the consumer with regard to the product items concerned. By gradation the product item may fall into a particular price range and the consumers will be prepared to accept the product within that range only.

3

Finance for Marketing

Finance is the essential input behind every managerial function, so also in marketing. The effective performance of marketing function invariably depends on the financial facility available with the marketer. Marketer takes every care in estimating the financial requirement on various fronts. Usually the financial requirement from the marketing point of view can be brought under two heads viz.,

1. Short term financial requirements
2. Long term financial requirements

Short Term Marketing Financial Requirements

Usually marketing is concerned with both short term as well as long term activities. Short term marketing financial requirement is concerned with the finance required to perform the marketing operations within one accounting year or even less than that period. Usually the short term finance constitutes as the working capital for performing marketing activities of the organisation concerned. The short term activities focus mainly on the execution of the planned marketing operations. The need for short term financial requirement emerges from the following major events :

1. Marketing administration
2. Transportation
3. Packaging
4. Commission
5. Interest
6. Market surveys
7. Publicity
8. Salesmen compensation

9. Storage
10. Ware houses
11. Test marketing
12. Additional offers
13. Modification of retail outlet
14. Administrative of retail outlet
15. Communication expenses
16. After sale service expenses

These expenses are to be met on routine basis and the extent of requirement of finance for these activities depends on the following factors :

* Nature of business
* Nature of market
* Volume of sales
* Type of sales
* Type of customer
* Terms of sales
* Terms of payment
* Operating cycle
* Seasonality
* Cost of production
* Nature of industry
* Stock turnover

Sources Providing Short Term Marketing Finance

The sources providing short term marketing finance are discussed below :

Trade Credit

Trade credit means the credit that customer gets from suppliers in the normal course of business. This is a type of deferred payment. Small firms particularly depends upon these types of finance for their day to day operation. Major advantage of this credit is easy availability and flexibility. Thus the trade credit is very informal. Trade credit also takes in the form of bills payable or accounts payable in a specified future date.

Advances from Customers

Advances from customers also serves as the essential means of working capital. Depending on the nature of product, its demand conditions and the terms of sales a firm can obtain advances from customers and that will constitute as the source for meeting short term requirements. Advances act as a free of cost source of finance.

Short Term Borrowings

Short term borrowings from institutions serve as another source of working capital finance. There are many institutions which render short term credit support and banks are usually one among those institutions. Banks of late started extending liberal working capital finance subject to the limit and conditions they stipulate. Banks mode of finance will take place in the form of overdraft. In case of overdrafts firms are allowed to withdraw funds in excess of the balances in their current account upto a specific period. The overdraft is subject to certain percentage of interest. The other forms of financing is cash credit.

Under the cash credit method the borrower is allowed to withdraw funds from the bank upto a sanctioned credit limit. The borrower is not expected to utilise the entire sanctioned credit limit. The borrower is not expected to utilise the entire sanctioned credit immediately rather the amount can be withdrawn whenever the requirement arises. Yet another way of working capital financing is purchasing or discounting of bills whereby the firm obtain credit against the bills. However the amount extended will be well within the overall cash credit or overdraft limit. Before purchasing or discounting the bills the bank has to satisfy itself as to the credit worthiness of the drawer and the bank holds the bill as the security for the credit. In addition to all these firms can opt for adhoc or temporary accommodation in excess of the sanctioned credit limit to meet unforeseen contingencies.

Accrued Expenses and Deferred Income

Accrued expenses represent a liability that firm has to pay for benefits that has been already received. It serves as a continuous interest free source of finance. Usually components of accrued income are wages, salaries interest etc.

Deferred income on the other hand represents funds received by the firms for goods and services which it has agreed to deliver at some future date. These receipts increases the firms liquidity in the form of cash therefore they constitute an important source of short term finance.

Long Term Marketing Financial Requirements

Long term marketing finance refers and include such of those financial requirements for a period of more than an accounting year to meet permanent long term expenses. The long term financial requirements for performing marketing function arises out of the following major events.

* Product planning and development
* Marketing research
* Market communication system
* Exploring new markets
* Export marketing
* Formation of marketing strategy
* Market expansion
* Product positioning
* New product development
* Product line expansion
* Establishment of retail outlets
* Fixation of wholesale distribution arrangements
* Establishment of retail outlets
* Establishment of warehouses
* Transportation system
* Establishment of after sales service network.

Factors Determining Long Term Marketing Finance

The long term financial requirement of a business firm is determined by considering, various activities involved in the functions such as production as well as marketing. The difficulty associated with estimation of long term finance is that the fixed assets are commonly used both by production as well by marketing and other related functionaries. Hence arriving at a compartmentalized allotment of long term finance in tune with the specific functions is rather difficult attempt. However the following lines summarize the factors that usually governs the long term financial requirement from the marketing functions point of view.

* Size of the business
* Type of technology employed
* Scale of operation
* Size of market share
* Method of distribution
* Building requirement
* Infrastructure build-up such as warehouse, storage and transportation

The major sources for the long term finances usually.

1. Shares
2. Debentures
3. Leasing
4. Term loans

Shares

Shares constitute as a major source of long term finance. Recently dependence on issue of shares for long term finance is on the increase. Company's resorted to this mode of financing, for the reasons such as easy public acceptance, it act as a source of permanent capital etc. Share is defined as a residual of the ownership. The shareholders have a claim over the earnings of the firm after paying expenses interest charges, taxes and preference dividend if any. The residual income may be divided into two parts namely dividend and retained earnings. Dividends are immediate cash flows to share holders. Retained earning are reinvested in the business and the share holders stand to benefit in the future date. The shares may be equity shares or preference shares. Shares are also divided into various other types depending on the specific features associated.

Debentures

The term debentures refers usually to long term bonds issued by the company for inviting the general public to contribute loan. The buyer of debentures are called debenture holders. The debenture holders are entitled for interest which is fixed and known. A debenture may be secured and unsecured which are subject to be reduced within a stipulated period. Of late the companies started issuing convertible debentures. A convertible debenture is one which can be converted fully or partly in to shares at a specified price at a given date. The most notable feature of the convertible debenture is that it promises a fixed income as well as the conversion option. Because of this reason a convertible debenture is called as hybrid security. The conversion value of a convertible debenture is equal to the conversion price multiplied by the common shares market price. The important reason behind issuing convertible debentures are it makes the issue attractive with payment of low interest rate. It stands as a deferred equity payment. Moreover convertible debentures serves as a low cost capital.

Leasing

Lease is a contract between lessor—(the owner of the asset), and a lesser—(the user of the asset). The lessee pays the rent to the lessor as a regular fixed payments over a period of time. A lessee may be an individual or a firm interested in the use of an asset without owning the same. The lessor may be equipment manufacturers or leasing companies who bring together the manufacturers and users. There are two types of leases.

Operating Lease : It is a short term, cancellable lease. Convenience and instant services are been provided by this type of operating lease.

Financial Lease : Long term, non cancellable lease contracts are known as financial lease. In India financial leases are very popular in case of high cost and highly technological equipments. Financial leases amortise the cost of asset over the term of lease. Financial lease avoid purchase price. Also it is to be noted that tax shields are available only when the company pays tax's leasing is a convenient and flexible method of financing. It lead to shifting of the risk of obsolescence.

Term Loans

Term loans represent long-term with a maturity of more than one year. Such credits are obtained from banks and specially created financial institutions. Such term loans are generally for a long period ranging from five years to twenty five years or more. These term loans are always secured. They are secured specially by the assets acquired using term loan funds. In addition to security of asset lender would like to protect himself further. As a result a number of covenants such as asset-related, liability related, cash flow related and control related are constituted. Asset related covenants are restrictions to maintain minimum working capital in terms of minimum current ratio. Liability related covenants stands for restrictions from incurring additional liability. The cash flow related covenants aims at restriction of firms cash outflow by means of dividend revenue expenditure and so on. The control related covenant refers to the organizational control by means of efficient managerial personnel. Usually commercial banks and financial institutions such as industrial finance corporation, industrial credit and investment corporation of India, Industrial Development Bank of India, Life Insurance Corporation, Unit Trust of India and so on, are engaged in extending term loan.

Financing for Specific Marketing Events

Financing for Product Development and Positioning

The successful development of product and its positioning in the market requires effective financial planning. The availability of finance has important implications over the product mix, product line and product related decisions. Product development and positioning involves the following activities :

* Product research
* Product designing
* Test marketing
* Product modification
* Product positioning

From the viewpoint of marketing concept the idea for product emanate from the identified needs of the consumers.

Identification of need and the related issues depend on the financial availability. Usually companies devote liberal financial sanction to product development as it is the first step towards many further steps in the marketing process. The product mix of a company consists of following four categories of product.

Question Marks

This types of products refer to that products which are having low growth rate, trying to enter into a market where there is already a market leader. The company has to dispense substantial money to keep up with the fast growing market.

Star Products

Refers to high growth share products which may or may not be self sufficient in respect of cash generation. Star product has a substantial market growth and company has to spend substantial fund in order to facilitate to grow further in the market.

Cash Cows

Cash cows brings large amount of cash inflow to the company. The company does not have to finance abundantly. Cash cows product enjoy market leader position and economics of operation.

Dogs

These types of product generate low profit or losses. The company should think critically in spending money on such product items. Generally these products will take away much money than what they actually deserve.

The product planning and development involves the following functions.

1. Idea Generation

It is a stage wherein the idea for new product is stimulated by means of techniques such as brain storming, Fantasy forced relationship and so on.

2. Idea Screening

This stage is concerned with critical appraisal of the idea generated in terms of its marketing goal opportunity and the like.

3. Business Analysis

In this stage thc idea is analysed in terms of its contribution to over all company and marketing objectives.

4. Product Development

At this stage the company produces a prototype product concept, manufacturing methods will be subject to serious research and further modifications. The product development has to undergo various stages which are dealt in detail already.

5. Test Marketing

Test marketing is concerned with the crucial stage of introducing the product in a selected market segment and understanding the reaction of that segment towards various attributes of the product. The response evoked from the test marketing may be of three types viz (i) Good, (ii) Fair, (iii) Poor. A 'good' response will lead to the introduction of the product, whereas a *'fair'* response will lead to either introduction or modification of the product. As regards the 'poor' response is concerned the company has to drop or modify the product. Wherever modification is done the test marketing will be repeated and the response are to be analysed before making an ultimate product launch.

6. Commercialisation

It is a stage of ultimate introduction of the product in the market. Marketing strategies already planned are to be implemented at this stage.

All the above stages explained are to be supported by means of enough finance. In fact finance play crucial role in each stage, from idea generation to commercialisation. The financial availability ultimately decide the sequence of each step. The company has to invest as well as expend sizable money for which no return is reaped until the product is accepted and sales takes place. Therefore financial resource is to be generated to nurture the product through the various stages.

At the commercialisation stage also the product has to undergo its lifecycle which has the stages of introduction, growth, maturity, saturation and decline.

At the introduction stage the sales of the product will be low leading to less cash generation. But in the mean time much cash has to be expended in the promotional activities of the product concerned. The position will improve only in growth stage where there will be fair return on investment and the cash generation may be sufficient enough to meet the expenditure related to the product. The financial condition will be unsatisfactory during the decline stage, where the product tend to loose its acceptance from the potential buyers, as a result inflow cash will be diminished.

Obviously the financial inflow towards product planning and development is identified with the type of product and its lifecycle in the market.

Brand Positioning

Brand positioning is concerned with findings a place for the brand in the mind of the prospective buyers. Every marketer is particular about positioning his brand by following appropriate strategy. Such strategy essentialy involve aspects such as market segmentation, product differentiation, building of brand image and so on. Each of the above aspects involve huge amount of monetary commitment.

Usually a company will allocate sizable amount from the total allocation for marketing to brand positioning. The financial allotment is made in such a way that the position of brand brings the expected perception in the mind of the target consumers. Brand position also enables, to refer the essence of brand in terms of its functional and non functional benefits.

Positioning of a brand in the consumer market is challenging and tough job, in view of competition. Product positioning demands financial commitment to perform the following events, very effectively. Such events are :

- Market segmentation
- Test marketing

- Product differentiation
- Communication
- Launching

Product positioning is closely linked with market segmentation. Market segmentation is the process of demassification of the total heterogeneous market of different characteristics into homogeneous market of uniform characteristics. Segmentation strategy includes identification of mass market, determination of suitable basis for segmentation and then segmenting the market. The segmented market will have influence over the costituents of the components of the marketing mix. The usual basis for market segmentation are as follows

Basis for Segmentation

Demographic	Geographic	Psychographic	Product
Age	Nation	Social class	Amount of usage
Sex	Region	Personality	Type of usage
Buying power	District	Life style	Brand loyalty
Expenditure patterns	State		Benefits sought
Occupation	City		
Education	Population density		
Nationality			
Family Life cycle			

The market segmentation above involves huge outflow of finance. As the segmentation form the basis for target market great caution is to be exercised in this regard.

The approach of segmentation essentially involves greater extent of financial outflow and that form part of the expenses of product positioning.

Financing for Distribution

Distribution is the corefunction of marketing. Performance of distribution function enables the movement of goods from the production center to the consumption centre. Effective distribution invariably requires a well framed distribution network. Distribution network is the arrangement between intra-company systems and extra company agents. The intra company system includes the quantity of production, the sequence of production, nature of production, available man power, transportation,. finance, storage and ware houses and the like. The extra company agencies include wholesalers, retailers and other middlemen. A company may resort to any level of distribution channel ranging from zero level to a level with two or more intermediaries. There are many factors that influence the channel choice and finance is one such important factor. From the viewpoint of distribution function finance has a definite role. The essentiality of finance function arise out of the performance of the following distribution related activities.

1. Identification of distribution channel
2. Fixation of distribution outlets
3. Conduct of pre-market survey to assess the effectiveness of distribution channel
4. Interior decoration of show rooms
5. Effective window display
6. Sales person's appointment and Remuneration
7. Storage and warehousing
8. Transportation
9. Publicity
10. Point of purchase display
11. Distribution related communication
12. Expenses for receiving and procuring orders.

In addition to the regular activities above, during seasonal as well as special occasions marketer has to make additional financial commitments. The extent of financial requirement for distribution function is determined by the following factors.

* Size of the market share
* Pattern of distribution
* Number of customers

* Type of customers
* Geographical location of the customers
* Nature of the product
* Value of the product
* Competitors distribution strategy
* Amount of communication required.

The financial requirement can be categorized as fixed and variable. The fixed expenditure is concerned with permanent long term expenditure in relation to establishment of distribution network and variable expenditure are those which are concerned with maintaining the distribution network in such a way that it contributes effectively towards the distribution objectives and thereby the overall marketing objectives.

The budgetary allocation of distribution objective will be determined by marketer taking into account of

* Nature and level of distribution
* Sales quota to be achieved and
* The overall distribution objectives

Usually the financial aspects relating to distribution is dealt by the concerned area sales manager in consultation with marketing officials and this is to a greater extent depends on the nature of organisation structure and the extent of the duties delegated and responsibilities assumed.

A proforma of distribution accounting statement is presented below

Distribution accounting statement : Area based/ Area

	Source	I	II	III	IV	Total
I	Distribution amount allotted	xxx	xxx	xxx	xxx	
II	Application					
	A. Fixed expenses					
	B. Variable expenses					
	Total					
	Surplus/Deficit					

Similarly the distribution accounting statement can be prepared on product basis, customer basis or any other suitable basis the organisation may require.

Financing for Promotion

In marketing, promotion assumes much significant role. It is ultimately the sales promotion efforts that help to reach the marketing goals in terms of product position, retainment and expansion.

Promotion mix which is an element of the marketing mix involves a blend of several components, mainly :

- Advertising
- Personal selling
- Public relations
- Publicity
- Other promotion measures

Financial decisions pertaining to the above components of promotion mix deserve utmost attention of the marketing strategists on several counts.

The decision on the components of the promotion mix takes into account of the following aspects

1. Product related aspects

The type of the product, its share in the market, the complex nature of the product, the unique sales proposition associated, the extent of differentiation, the expected sales volume stage in the life cycle are matters affecting the financial policy decision for promotion.

2. Market related aspects

The market related aspects are concerned with market share, market leader or follower position and the like.

3. Consumer related aspects

The consumer aspects are those which are concerned with the number of consumers, their socio economic status geographical distribution, Lifestyle, family size and so on.

4. Communication related aspects

The communication related aspect is concerned with media availability, extent of coverage, the cost of each media, competitors media and so on.

5. Company related aspects

The company related aspects are those concerned with the objectives of the company, the marketing goods and the related aspects.

Promotion Strategy

A firm may adopt three types of strategies viz (i) a push strategy (ii) a pull strategy (iii) and a gravity strategy. A regards push strategy the producer will push the product to the wholesaler, the wholesaler will push it to the retailer and retailer will ultimately push the product to the consumer. Push strategy usually is concerned with the personal selling force. A pull strategy involves focus on the promotional efforts direct on the ultimate consumers rather than the middlemen. As such pull strategy involves heavy spending on advertising directed towards the ultimate consumers. The gravity strategy on the other hand deals with concentrating on producing a superior product and depending only on the buyers of that superior product to convey their extent of satisfaction to others, which will induce others to buy. A firm which lacks funds for other methods of sales promotion may resort to this type of sales promotion.

Based on the above aspects the financial outlay for the promotion programme would be streamlined. Such streamlined outlay will be distributed among the components of the various promotion mix, in tune with their relative significance in the promotion strategy. The financial implication and related aspects with regard to major components of the promotion mix is detailed below :

Financial Allocation for Promotion

The financial allocation for the promotion expenditure will be normally for one accounting year. The budgeted financial allocation for promotion will incorporate budget for advertising, personal selling, public relation and for other sales promotion measures.

The proforma of financial outlay statement is present below:

Financial Outlay Statement for Promotional Activities

Promotion Component	Jan-Mar (Rs)	Apr-July (Rs)	July-Sep (Rs)	Oct-Dec (Rs)
Advertising				
Personal selling				
Public relations				
Sales promotion				
Total				

The above financial outlay statement may take place in the forms such as product wise or market segment wise or in a matrix form depending on the specific requirement of the firm concerned.

Consideration for Allocation of Finance for Promotional Activities

The financial allocation for the promotional activities is made after giving due consideration on the following lines.

1. Analysis of Past Data

A thorough analysis of past data relating to market conditions, consumer behaviour, media choice, media effectiveness, competitors behaviour, previous financial outlay made and the future changes forecasted on these aspects are to be analysed.

2. The Duration

Usually the allocation of finance for promotion is for a period of one year. However the benefit cannot be reaped within one year, which is going to be carried to many forthcoming years which cannot be specified. As such the promotional finance allocation as well as settlement of allocation cannot be determined well in advance in a accountable manner.

Position of the Firm

The position of the firm in terms of its earnings, reserves etc., are other aspects that limits the financial allocation. Usually the financial position will have a direct impact on the expenses for promotion. It is believed that the accumulated spending will yield continuous benefit.

Competitor Role

The competitor's financial outlay for the year is another point before the firm could take à final decision on its financial outlay. For many companies competitors financial outlay for promotion expenditure is the basis of their own allotment.

The Position in Product Life Cycle

Product life cycle is concerned with the following stages viz.,

1. Introduction
2. Growth
3. Maturity
4. Saturation and
5. Decline

A product item may fall into any one of the five stages in the product life cycle. At the introductory stage higher amount of financial commitment is needed for promotional expenses to make the product introduced and accepted. In case of growth and maturity stages wider consumer acceptance will lead to more sales with less amount of promotional expenditure. At the decline stage only less investment in promotional expenditure will be made as there is a resistance towards acceptance of the product item in view of competitors product or due to technological upgradation of similar product item or due to changes in life style of the consumer as the case it may be. Apparently it shows that the position of the product in the life cycle plays a decisive role in determining the financial outlay for promotional expenditure.

Methods of Financial Outlay for Promotion

The following are the basis available to determine the financial outlay :

1. Subjective Budgeting Basis

Under this method executives concerned decide the allocation of fund to over all promotion as well as to the components on the basis of personal judgment. The method is not scientific. Past experience is the only guidance in determining as well as allocating the amount. More risk is assumed in this subjective budgeting basis.

2. Percentage on of Sale Basis

Under this method a specific percentage is allocated by taking the expected sales into consideration. The expected sales is projected by means of appropriate technique. Based on past experience a specific percentage on sale is allotted for the promotion expenditure. This method is easy to understand and also based on logical reasoning.

3. Objective Task Basis

Under this method the promotion objective will be set first. Based on the same, the objective of the components will be laid. The promotional objective, however depend on the over all marketing objective. For example if the companies over all marketing goal is to increase its market share by 4% and the promotion objective will be determined as to encourage retailers to increase the stocking of product by 20% in the retail out let. Accordingly the promotional expenditure will be fixed as below.

	Previous year Rupees (%)	Current year Rupees (%)
Advertising	20	28
Personal selling	20	28
Sales promotion	40	56
Public relation	20	28
Total promotional expenses	100	140

An over all increase of 4% in the component is noticeable. The percentage is however fixed by means of product-by-product or market-by-market through analysis.

The method of financial outlay however demand high sense of judgment analysis, and forecast is obviously necessary. In tune with the changing market conditions the promotional expenses must also vary to keep and expand the stand in the market. In order to enable uncertainties "promotional contingencies fund" is preferred. Such contingency fund will enable to adjust unforeseen uncertainties.

Accounting for Promotional Expenses

The promotional expenses may be classified and accounted under two heads namely variable and fixed expenses. The promotion expenses are usually brought under the heads of product items, or sales territory. The classification of promotional expenses as to fixed and variable is crucial and complex. With respect to promotion department the items then can be classified as variable are as below :

1. Department travel expenses
2. Entertainment expenses
3. Salaries expenses
4. Association expenses
5. Subscription to periodicals and journal
6. Stationeries and office supplies
7. Charges of services performed other department
8. Charges to vehicles
9. Incidental charges to buildings
10. Rental charges
11. Subscriptions
12. Storage charges of advertising materials
13. Department share of overload expenses
14. Employee benefits
15. Entertainment to customers

On the other hand the fixed charges pertaining to promotion are as below :

1. Payment to advertising agents
2. Pre testing charges
3. Media costs
4. Readership/audience research
5. Direct mail to consumers

6. Sponsorship charges
7. Catalogs for consumers
8. Classified telephone directories
9. Promotions aids to salesman
10. Dealer help literature
11. Point of sales materials
12. Window displays installation charges
13. Cost of exhibition trade fair
14. Cost of exhibits
15. Catalogs for salesman
16. Consumer contest awards
17. Expenditure on tie-in-promotions
18. Consumer education programs
19. Supply of samples
20. Personnel recruitment expenditure
21. Charities
22. Sponsorship
23. Donation

There is no hard and fast rule as to the classification of the promotion expenditure into fixed or variables. There are many expenditure which assume the characteristics of partly variable also. Such classifications depends on the nature of organisation their accounting policy and practice.

The accounting statement showing promotional expenditure is shown below :

Accounting Statement of Promotional Expenses

	Jan-Mar	Apr-June	July-Sept	Oct-Dec
	Rs.	Rs.	Rs.	Rs.
Gross margin				
Less Variable expenses				
Advertising				
1				
2				
3				

(contd...)

	Jan-Mar	Apr-June	July-Sept	Oct-Dec
	Rs.	Rs.	Rs.	Rs.
4				
5	xxx	xxx	xxx	xxx
Personal selling	xxx	xxx	xxx	xxx
1				
2				
3	xxx	xxx	xxx	xxx
	xxx	xxx	xxx	xxx
Sales promotion				
1				
2				
3	xxx	xxx	xxx	xxx
	xxx	xxx	xxx	xxx
Public relation				
1				
2				
3	xxx	xxx	xxx	xxx
Less : Fixed expenses	xxx	xxx	xxx	xxx

The above statement may be prepared on product wise, or marketer segment wise or any other basis, suits to the particular organisation concerned and accordingly suitable modification in the statement be incorporated.

Financing for Export Marketing

Export marketing of an organisation leads to interaction with overseas business firms and also with the international environment. The market ecology with reference to export market comprises the following factors.

I. Political and Demographic

Power structure in the society
Density and distribution of population
Legal system
Government policy
Role of ethnic group
Military aspects

II. Socio economic

Level of disposable per capita income
Centres of purchasing influence
New industrial development source
Availability of mobility of labour
Distribution of income
Structure of social class
Government fiscal policies

III. Cultural factors

Educational level
Level of technical and managerial ability
Language
Status of women
Material culture
Religious belief
Reference group of buyers
Consumption system
Aesthetics

IV. Geographical/Environmental

Communication system
Climatic and topography
Proximately of source
Logistic system

A marketer entering into export has to necessarily take into account of the above factors to design the export market plan and strategy.

Finance from the export marketer's viewpoint is the key factor limiting the strategic framework of the export operations. The export operation incorporate the following levels :

1. Identifying and measuring market opportunities
2. Developing export marketing strategy
3. Operational aspect of export

Among other things, the financial aspect involved in all the above levels determine the efficiency of the organisation in respect of its export performance.

The financial requirement for export operation can be summarised under two stages.

* Preshipment finance
* Post shipment finance

Preshipment finance

Preshipment finance is concerned with financial requirements, until the product reaches the sales destination. The preshipment credit is also called as packing credit. Post shipment finance on the other hand is concerned with the financial requirement marketing operations starting with the entry of the product at the export destination until it reaches the ultimate buyer.

The extend of need for export finance is determined by the following factors.

1. Efforts for Exploring Expc Potential

This is a primary step in export market operations. The product having export potential has to undergo an exploration process involving identification of international trade policies, agreements, concerned with the international treaty organizations. International bodies like world bank, GATT, IMF also play significant role in the exploration process.

2. Contact Agencies

The second factor that determines the preshipment finance is the expenses associated with contact sources. Contact sources is to be identified, screened and ultimately selected. This process involves considerable financial commitment. The usual contact sources are :

* Overseas agents
* Export service and promotion divisions
* Banks
* Local government industrial ministry
* Overseas government industrial and commerce ministry
* Chamber of commerce
* Trade fair authorities
* Specialised agencies
* Professional institutions

* Industrial export councils
* Personal contact
* Other exporters
* Research organisation and the like.

3. Developing Export Accessibility

Export accessibility being developed by means of effective communication, personal visit and creating exchange relationship. This is a crucial stage and this also has a role in determining the size of preshipment financial requirement. Export access will render thorough knowledge on export policy, licensing, tariff system, customes, exchange rates, determination and other regulations.

4. Product Designing and Development

Product development depends on the level of the target country's level of economic development. The product development and the economic position has to go together so that the chance for exportability will be more. The following matrix explain the relationship.

Market aggregates	Product configuration	Standard product	More sophistication	More basic product
* Industrial countries				
* Semi industrial countries				
* New industrial countries				
* Developed countries				
* Under-developed countries				

According to the market aggregate the product configuration is to be arranged or vice versa. A considerable amount of finance has to be necessarily allocated in this process.

5. Storage and Warehouse

Storage and warehouse arrangements also determine the preshipment finance. The product meant for shipment is to be kept ready in the storage. Depending on the tariff rate, period of storage, nature of storage and the like.

6. Work Force Management

Overseas operation requires effective manpower planning and management. Overseas marketing identifies with national marketing in many respects, but in the meantime it involves much more extensive way of performance of marketing operation which require effective work force. The exporting firm has to essentially allocate funds for work force planning, recruitment, selection, training, and to control them also.

7. Distribution Network

The method of distribution is another factor influencing the financial requirements. Depending on the nation's distribution practice as well as the facilities available, distribution network varies. Accordingly the cost of distribution also varies, which influences the extent of financial requirement.

8. Sales Promotion Measures

Sales promotion activity involves advertising, publicity, personal selling and other sales promotion measures including public relation and these items has a role in deciding the extent of export financial requirement.

9. Overseas Administrative Overhead

Overseas administrative overhead takes into account all that expenses necessary to perform smooth export operation.

Preshipment Finance

Methods of preshipment finance include

1. Letter of credit
2. Packing credit

Letter of Credit

Letter of credit is defined by the International Chamber of Commerce as any arrangement however named or described whereby an issuing bank acting at the request and in accordance with the instruction of a customer.

1. to make a payment to or to the order of third party or to pay, accept or negotiate bills of exchange drawn by beneficiary or
2. authorise another bank to effect such bill of exchange against stipulated documents provided that the terms and conditions of credit are complied with.

Types of Letter of Credit

The letter of credit is usually divided under two heads. Personal letter of credit and Commercial letter of credit.

Personal letter of credit is otherwise known as encashment credit whereby one banker request another banker to whom the said letter is addressed to hold a certain sum to the disposal of a third person who is the holder of the letter and to pay him such amount as he requires against cheque.

Letter of commercial credit on the other hand is used for the purpose of financing shipment of goods imported into or exported from a country for movement of produce from one place to another.

The following are the various types of commercial letter of credit.

Revocable and Irrevocable Letter of Credit

In case of revocable or unconfirmed letter of credit a banker issuing them can cancel the authority at any time he chooses but he will still liable for bills negotiated before its cancellation. A irrevocable or confirmed letter of credit cannot be cancelled unless it has run its full course or unless its beneficiary agrees for such cancellation.

Documentary Letter of Credit or Clean Letter of Credit

A clean letter of credit is that which incorporate a clause regarding tittle to goods such as bill of lading, insurance policy, consular invoice, certificate of origin etc. If a letter of credit does not contain any such clause it is called clean letter of credit.

Fixed Credit and Revolving Credit

If the letter of credit contains specification as regards the maximum amount within a specified period of time i.e., termed as fixed letter of credit. On the other hand if the banker does not specify the total amount upto which bill may be drawn is revolving letter of credit. However in case of the revolving letter of credit the total amount upto which bill drawn may remain outstanding for a time which will be specified.

With and Without Recourse

In case of with recourse, the banker as the holder of the bill, can recover the amount of the bill from its drawer, if the drawee fails to honour it. In order to avoid such liability the exporter may ask the importer to arrange credit without recourse to the drawer. Under this type of credit the issuing banker will have recourse to the drawee and if he fails to honour the bill, the banker can realize the amount by disposing of goods.

Transferable and Non Transferable Letter of Credit

Under a transferable letter of credit the beneficiary can transfer his right to draw a bill to another person. A transferable credit is a credit under which the beneficiary has right to give instruction to the bank called upon to effect payment or acceptance, or to any bank entitled to effect negotiation to make the credit available in whole or in part to one or more of third parties. In case of the letter of credit if it is not transferable it is called in transferable letter of credit.

Back to Back Letter of Credit

When a beneficiary receives a non transferable letter of credit he may request the bank to open new letter of credit in favour of some other person on the security of letter of credit issued in his favour, such letter of credit is called back to back letter of credit.

Red Clause Letter of Credit

A red clause letter of credit contains an authority from the issuing banker to the advising or negotiating banker to grant advances to the beneficiary upto a specified amount at the responsibility of the former. The advance made under this letter of credit is for a short period and is recovered from the amount payable by the negotiating banker to the beneficiary when the later negotiates the required documents under the letter of credit.

Letter of credit, thus serves as a source of finance by facilitating certainty of payment, avoidance of risk, security against exchange restrictions and as a provision for advance payment.

Post Shipment Finance

Post shipment finance refers to any type of finance extended by an institution to an exporter from the date after the shipment of goods to the date of realization of export proceeds and includes any loan or advance granted to the exporter for consideration like security or incentives from government.

The Types of Post Shipment Finance

The post shipment finance include :

a. Payment/acceptance of export document
b. Purchase for discount under confirmed order
c. Advances against bills sent on collection basis
d. Advances against undrawn balances
e. Advances against cash incentives
f. Advances against duty draw back entitlement
g. Advances against retention money
h. Financing export under deferred payment arrangement

Institutions Involved in Export Finance

Reserve Bank of India :

The RBI extends various financial support schemes for export promotion through its industrial and export credit development source. Some important schemes of RBI are :

a. Export Credit (Interest Subsidy) Scheme

Under this scheme the banks are allowed to extend on stipulated conditions export credit on concessional terms to the exporter and in return they can claim subsidy from RBI.

b. Bill Market Scheme

Rediscounting facilities are being offered under this scheme. RBI refinance to eligible commercial banks against their declaration of export bills drawn in foreign or Indian currencies.

c. Preshipment Credit Refinance Facility

Under this scheme, refinance facility is allowed to the banks so as to enable them to extend financial facility to exporter.

EXIM Bank

The EXIM bank provides financial assistance to exporters and importers. It coordinate the other institution's operations functioning for the purpose of providing of export as well as import finance. The lending program of EXIM bank include direct financial assistance, Technology consultancy services, overseas investment financing, preshipment credit, export product development assistance, export marketing fund.

Commercial Banks

Commercial banks render usually three types of functions :

1. Transfer function

Which facilitate payments without the medium of currency through various credit instrument.

2. Credit function

It involves credit facilities to preshipment and post shipment through bill of exchange or letter of credit and so on.

3. Hedging function

Involves forward purchase and sales of foreign currency for eliminating the risk of fluctuations in exchange.

Export Credit Guarantee Corporation of India Ltd.

The ECGC has designed, several policies to suit every type of export transaction. ECGC provides export credit insurance and guarantee facilities to Indian exporters. The shipment (comprehensive risks) policy covers commercial risks and political risks, the schemes offered by each include specific policies. They are designed to protect Indian firms against payment risks in a deferred payment.

Financial Guarantees

Guarantees issued to banks in India to protect them from the risk of loss involved in extending financial support to exporters at preshipment and postshipment stages.

Special Schemes

These are meant to protect banks which are acting on letter of credit opened by foreign banks, overseas investment insurance and exchange fluctuation risk insurance.

The Industrial Credit and Investment Corporation of India

The export finance extended by ICICI induces

1. Long term rupee loans and foreign currency loans
2. Funding of exports including grants for productivity improvement
3. Lease finance for domestic and imported equipment
4. Finance for technology advancement.

Special Financial Schemes for Exports

1. Buyers Credit Scheme

The EXIM bank operates the buyer credit scheme which envisages grant of credit by EXIM bank in participation with commercial banks to the foreign buyer for export of capital goods. The scheme provides for payment to be made to exporters out of buyers credit on a non-recourse basis on themselves fulfilling the commercial terms of the export contract to be financed. The exporters competence, commercial justification of contract, economic viability are to be considered for the purpose of buyers credit. Before extending buyers credit, it is necessary to obtain permission under Foreign Exchange Regulation Act (FERA), as it is extended to foreign buyers.

2. EXIM Lines of Credit

The EXIM bank extend lines of credit to the foreign governments or its agents to enable them to buy capital or engineering goods from India on deferred payment scheme. This facility is available to sovereign governments or agencies nominated by them.

3. Forfeiting

Forfeiting is emerging as a new concept of export financing. This enables an exporter to offer deferred credit to overseas importer. It may be in the form of

1. without recourse to the exporter
2. fixed interest rate of finance
3. discounting of bill of exchange
4. Guarantee by banks

The basic objective of forfeiting is payment of the instruments like promissory note or bill of exchange to the exporter without recourse to any previous holder of the instrument. Forfeiting is appropriate to medium and large scale export contracts.

Consumer Finance

The decision with respect to purchase or otherwise of a product is ultimately bound by the financial position of the consumer. A marketer in today's competitive marketing environment must focus attention on the financial position of the target buyer. This will serve as one of the major considerations for decisions pertaining to the components of the marketing mix.

The financial position of the consumer is governed by three types of expenses viz. discretionary, partly discretionary and, non discretionary expenses. A discretionary expense is that which is incurred at the discretion of the consumer. Expenses on entertainment, travelling, ornaments, charity, incidental expenses, expenses on luxury items etc. are examples for discretionary expenses as there is no compulsion to expend on such items. Contrary to this, non discretionary expenses include the expenses that the consumer has to necessarily spend without exercising his option for e.g., medical expenses, educational expenses, clothing, rent, taxes and other dues if any etc. The partly discretionary expenses are those which are concerned with amount to be set aside for savings. Insurance policies and so on depending on the voluntary commitment made by the consumer himself. The income statement of a consumer will appear as follows:

Income and Expenditure Statement

Sources of Income			
* Salary		xxx	
* Business		xx	
* Interest		xxx	
* Rent		xxx	
* Casual		xxx	
*		xxxx	
*Expenditure			
Non Discretionary			
* Education	xx		
* Medical	xx		
* Rent	xx		
* Interest	xx		
* Clothing	xx		
* Food	xx		
* Taxes	xx		
* Dues	xx		
* Other necessary expenses	xx	xxx	
Discretionary			
* Travelling	xx		
* Entertainment	xx		
* Charity	xx		
* Books/Magazine	xx		
* Other luxury	xx	xxx	
Partly Discretionary			
* Insurance	xx		
* Deposits	xx		
* Saving schemes	xx	xxx	xxxx
Deficit/Surplus			xxxx

The income and expenditure pattern of the target consumer is of pertinent consideration to the marketer as it will enable to arrive decision on the following issues

* What type of product will be preferred?
* What price the consumer can pay?
* The media of communication
* Nature of spending
* Collection method
* Future operations
* Package size
* Demand trend and so on.

In the context of consumer confronted, with limited spending power making him buy a product is a difficult aspect. Unless the consumer is left with financial means he will not come forward to make the purchase and the marketing efforts will not reach the goal. Today the marketers has to come forward not only to offer the product but also make effective means of source of finance. Such an arrangement of source of finance will itself induces the buyer to purchase without postponement for the non availability of finance. In this context consumer finance gains significance. Consumer finance refers to the finance obtained by the consumer for maintaining as well as increasing his present consumption. It is also called as consumer credit, which is meant for a short term period. The consumer finance is usually in the following forms.

(1) Charge Account

A charge account is otherwise called as open account credit. It is opened generally in the retail outlet. As and when the buyer buys the product the buyer will be charged with the amount. There will be an understanding between the retailer and the buyer as to the maximum amount of such credit and the period for which the buyer can avail the credit, the product that can be purchased etc. This type of credit may be open account or revolving account.

An open account is that in which the consumer pays the bill in full when it is due. Normally no interest is charged. A revolving account on the other hand refers to a buyer being charged with the prices of items during the month and he is billed at the end of the month. The buyer will usually pay a part of the amount on the basis of outstanding balances. The buyer will be usually charged with interest.

Example of Open Account	**Rs.**
Purchase in Jan 1-31	5000.00
Payment made in Feb 1st	5000.00
Balance due	Nil

Example of Revolving Account	**Rs.**
Purchase made in Jan 1-31	5000.00
Payment made 1st Feb	3800.00
Balance due	1200.00
Purchases Feb 1-29	3000.00
Interest for balance of Jan @ 10%	12.00
Balance due	4212.00
Payment made March 1st	4000.00
Balance due	212.00
Purchase made	5000.00
Interest for amount due in march	
$212 \times \frac{1}{12} \times \frac{10}{100}$	1.77
	5213.77

(2) Instalment Credit

Instalment credit is a long term consumer credit. This form is usually practiced when the consumer has to buy products which are relatively priced higher and the consumer is left with only part of the amount. Under this system the buyer is allowed to own the product by paying a initial payment which is known as down payment. The remaining price of the product along with interest is divided into a number of instalments which will be paid usually every month.

3. Hire Purchase Agreement

Under the Hire purchase agreement the seller agrees to transfer the possession of the product to buyer on receipt of a part of the price. However the ownership right is with the seller only until the buyer pays and the entire due.

The Hire Purchase Act, 1972 defines hire purchase as "an agreement under which goods are let on hire and under which the hirer has an option to purchase them in accordance with the terms of agreement and includes an agreement under which

1. Possession of the goods is by the owner thereof on condition that the owner pays the agreed amount in periodical instalment and
2. The property in the goods is to pass to such person on the payment of the last of such instalment

The hire purchase agreement usually include the following:

a. The hire purchase prices of goods to which the agreement relates.
b. The cash price i.e., to say the price at which the goods may be purchased by the hirer for cash.
c. The date on which the agreement deemed to have commenced.
d. The number of instalment by which the hire purchase price is to be paid.
e. The amount of each such instalment.
f. The date of payment, the person to whom the amount is payable, the place where payable.
g. The goods which agreement relates in manner sufficient to identify them.

Accounting for the Purchase and Instalment

The accounting procedure for hire purchase and instalment is briefed below :

The accounting procedure involves calculation of interest. One way of calculating the interest is to make a memorandum account of one of the parties, the seller or buyer. In a given case on Ist Jan 92 a product is purchased. The down payment being Rs.4000 and instalment @ Rs.4000 for three years. The cash price of the produce is Rs.14,900 and the interest rate is 5%. The interest can be calculated by means of preparation of hire vendor account as below :

Hire Vendors Account

1992				
Jan	To cash	4000	By product	14,900
Jan 31	To cash	4000	By interest 5% on 10,900	540
	To bal c/d	7445		
		15,445		15,445
1993				
Dec	To cash	4000	By bal b/c	7445
	To bal c/d	3817	By interest 5% on 7445	370
		7817		7817
1994				
Dec	To cash	4000	By bal b/d	3817
			By interest	183
		4000		4000

The total interest being 540 + 372 + 183 =1095

This accounting method is usually been practiced for the purpose of calculating interest rate.

For the purpose of calculation of cash price the usual model adopted will be

Rate of Interest

100 + Rate of interest

The cash price can also be calculated of the instalments are uniform by means of the following model

$$\frac{1 - \left(1 + \frac{r}{100}\right)^{n}}{\frac{r}{100}}$$

where 'r' is the rate of interest per annum

'n' is the number of year over which the payment is to be made.

In certain aspects the instalment credit and the hire purchase are one and the same. But both differ mainly on two fronts viz., (1) under instalment credit the ownership right is transferred along with the first payment whereas under hire purchase agreement the ownership right passes only when entire price is paid (2) In case of default, under instalment credit the seller can use in the court for the balance amount due. However under hire purchase system the seller will not transfer the ownership right and the amount paid which will be treated as hire charge.

Both these forms of consumer finance is found suitable for certain types of products which are highly priced, easily distinguishable, durable in nature and standardized.

In view of these types of consumer finance there is the possibility of widening the market by including those buyers who cannot make the payment at one time. However the noticeable drawback is that the seller has to maintain complete and accurate records pertaining to the amount due, payment made, interest changes, outstanding balances and so on.

Specialized Consumer Finance Schemes

Lending institutions has now come forward to extend consumer finance for a longer period for specialized purpose. Such purposes include acquisition of ownership of durable demanding huge instalments. Few example for consumer finance are :

* Housing financing
* Durable (Television, refrigerator etc.)

The lending institutions involved in specialized consumer finances are banks, private financial companies sellers, owned financial agencies, specialized agencies and so on. The method of operation of extension of specialized consumer finance with reference to housing finance is given below as a sample for specialized consumer finance.

Specialized Consumer Finance : A Sample Presentation with Reference to Housing Purposes

There are many agencies involved in extending housing financial support. The Life Insurance Housing Finance Ltd.,

Housing Development Finance Corporation Ltd., CANFIN Homes Ltd. and India Housing Finance Development Ltd. are some of the renowned agencies extending consumer finance for housing purpose.

The procedure adopted, the amount of financial support, terms of payment, criteria for sanctioning the finance etc are not uniform among all the agencies concerned. As regards Life Insurance Corporation, the consumer applying for the finance must be a Life insurance policy holder and or his immediate family should not own a house already. The consumer finance from LIC ranges between Rs.25,000 to Rs.500,000 and the repayment period is within 30 years or on superannuation of the person of on attainment of 65 years which ever is first. Life insurance offers consumer finance schemes like Jeevan Kulis and Jeevan Nivas. The loan granted under Jeevan Kulis ranges from Rs.25,000 to Rs.200,000 and under Jeevan Nivas the loan extended ranges from Rs.25,000 to Rs.500,000.

The Housing Development Finance Corporation also extends finance for housing purposes. The finance is provided for acquisition of self contained flats in an existing or proposed cooperative society. The financial limit sanctioned depends on the age, income, qualification, number of dependents, spouse income, asset, liability position and other related aspects. The minimum loan amount is Rs.7,500 and the maximum is Rs.500,000. The repayment period ranges from 5 to 20 years. Different housing finance schemes are available viz., House Loan scheme (individual). Line of Credit Facility (corporate) Home Extension Loan, Home Improvement Loan etc. The mode of repayment may be equated monthly instalment or step-up repayment facility. The security for the loan may be in the form of deposit deeds or such other collateral security.

The CANFIN Homes Limited is another unit sponsored by Canara Bank in association with Unit Trust of India. CANFIN usually extend financial support to individuals who do not own any house. The CANFIN loan is extended for a longer period ranging from 7 to 20 years of time. The consumer availing for such loan if salaried should have a minimum seven years service and if self employed should not be aged more than 58 years. The rate of interest ranges from 10% to 17% and the quantum of loan ranges from Rs.7,500 to Rs.5,00,000. Period of repayment of loan is fixed taking into account age and income of the consumers. The loan is repayable on equated instalments. The security for such finance is normally deposit deeds.

In India Housing and Development Ltd. also extends consumer finance for the purpose of housing. The loan sanctioned ranges from Rs.7,500 to Rs.5,00,000. The loan sanctioned may vary from 65% to 80% of the cost of the property including registered cost of the land. The interest rate usually calculated on the outstanding loan amount on annual rest. The repayment should made on equated monetary instalment comprising.

Credit Cards : A Source of Consumer Finance

Credit card is a mechanism of consumer finance that served equal to liquid cash subject to terms and conditions stipulated by the issuing authority, usually the commercial banks. The credit cards are plastic cards containing details such as name of the banker, name of the holder, number of the card, validity period, signature of the holder. Credit cards enable shopping and it avoids the risk of carrying cash. Some of the popular credit cards in India are CAN card (Canara Bank), BOB card (Bank of Baroda), IND card (Indian Bank), VISA card (City Bank), India card (Bank of India), SBI card (State Bank of India), Andhra Bank card (Andhra Bank), SBM card (State Bank of Mysore) and SBT card (State Bank of Travancore).

The credit cards are normally issued to individuals who are having honest dealings with the bank. Individuals who are not account holders but prominent people also will be issued with the credit cards. However Non Resident Indians should get the approval of Reserve Bank of India before obtaining credit cards.

The card holders should maintain sufficient balance in their operating account to cover all charges arising out of transactions through credit cards at the time of debiting the accounts. The cards holders are required to pay membership fee also.

Add-on facility is extended to family members of the credit card holders and seaport cards will be issued. All changes incurred by Add-on card holders will be included in the statement of main card holder and debit to his account.

The credit cards enable card holders to make purchases and avail services at various designated shops. All the shops who are accepting credit cards are called as member establishments.

The enlisted member establishment will enter into agreement with the bank. Thereby the terms and conditions of honouring the credit card will be fixed. Such agreement is subject to revision periodically. Cancellation of credit cards will take place when there is gross misutilisation of cards on account of insolvency/ death of card holders and many other reasons which result in loss to the bank.

Generally the card is property of the issuing bank and is to be returned to the bank on request. The bank is not responsible for any defective merchandise purchased and services availed by the card holder. The issuing bank reserves the right to renew at its discretion.

4

Marketing Cost Analysis

Marketing cost analysis involves breaking down and classifying marketing cost in order to determine the cost incurred in performing the marketing activity. Marketing cost analysis enables determination of marketing cost which will provide direction to the future course of action. In a broader sense marketing cost involves all these cost incurred in such of those marketing activities involved right from of consumer need identification to consumer need satisfaction. A detailed break up of marketing cost runs as below and each head constitute a cost centre.

* Market research
* Product development
* Package
* Test marketing
* Product launching
* Advertisement
* Personal selling
* After sale service
* Storage
* Transportation
* Insurance
* Grading
* Salary
* Commission
* Brokerage
* Others

The list of cost centres identified above may be expanded or contracted depending on the marketing pattern of the individual firm concerned.

The list above can be grouped under heads namely product cost, promotion cost, distribution cost and other functional cost.

The cost statement pertaining to marketing function will be as follows :

Marketing Cost Statement

	Rs.	Rs.
Sales		xxxx
Less		
Cost of goods sold :		
- Direct material	xxx	
- Direct labour	xxx	
- Direct expense	xxx	xxxx
Gross Margin		xxxxx
Less		
Marketing cost :		
Product cost		
- Product development	xx	
- Package	xx	
- Launching	xx	
		xx
Distribution cost		
- Storage	xx	
- Transport	xx	
- Insurance	xx	
- Grading	xx	
- Commission	xx	
- Brokerage	xx	
		xx
Promotion cost		
- Advertising	xx	
- Personal selling	xx	
- Other promotion methods	xx	
		xx

Other functional cost			
- Marketing research	xx		
- Test marketing	xx		
- Processing order	xx		
- After sales service	xx		
- Salary	xx	xx	xxxxxxx
Net Margin			xxxxxx

Marketing cost analysis provides the following values to the organization :

1. A detailed insight into the marketing cost structure.
2. Assigning specific responsibility to the respective functional heads in terms of cost benefits,
3. A comparative analysis spotlights efficiency associated with the performance in general.
4. Additional allocation and reallocation are made possible in tune with resource paucity.
5. Marketing cost effectiveness in terms of overall cost invoived can be determined and compared.

Marketing Cost Relationship Analysis

The marketing cost relationship analysis is pivotal because such analysis provide deep insight into the comparative efficiency of the cost incurred on various heads. The method of analysis is as below :

1. Analysis by comparing with competing firms.
2. Analysis by comparing with proceeding years
3. Analysis by comparing with expenses/income from other heads.

Analysis by comparing with other competing firms cost detail will enable to determine the comparative cost efficiency. However it depends upon the availability of factual details from comparative firms. While making such comparison care should be devoted to the distinctiveness associated with such firms with which the cost is compared and due allowances are to be administered for such distinctiveness. Also it is to be noted that the significance of each function may vary from firm to firm. The cost associated with the following heads can be generally compared.

- Selling and distribution cost
- Advertising
- Transportation
- Package
- Insurance etc.

Analysis by comparing the cost detail of preceding years is another method available to determine the cost efficiency. Accordingly the cost incurred to perform a specific function in the previous year is to be compared with the present year. Here efforts should be taken to eliminate abnormalities in the heads of expenses. Such abnormalities are to be duly dealt to arrive at normal situation to enable comparison.

The method of determining efficiency by comparing cost incurred under one head with that of other head is usually done by means of using ratio analysis. The details of ratio analysis are presented below :

Ratio Analysis in Relation to Marketing

Ratio is used as a index for evaluating the position as well as performance of a given item, in relation to another items. The relationship between two accounting figures, expressed mathematically is known as ratio. These ratios are used as standards for comparison. Comparison may be taken place within the firm itself with reference to previous year ratios or the performance of one firm with another firm within the industry.

As regards marketing functions are concerned the following ratios deserve significance.

- Advertising cost ratio
- Distribution cost ratio
- Transportation cost ratio
- Package ratio
- Insurance expense ratio
- Personal selling expense ratio
- After sales service expense ratio
- Product launching cost ratio
- Marketing research expense ratio

In all the above cases a particular head of expense is compared to sales volume and the ratio is thus arrived.

For e.g. Advertisement cost ratio $= \dfrac{\text{Advertisement cost}}{\text{Sales}} \times 100$

A company spends Rs. 30,000 during the month of January, 1993 and the sales volume for that year is 3,00,000. The advertising ratio worked to be

$$\frac{30{,}000}{300{,}000} \times 100 = 10\%$$

An analysis of this ratio reveals that for every Rs.10 spend on advertisement, the firm would make sales worth Rs.100. Comparison with previous years figure will throw light on the improving or declining level of sales efficiency. On the other hand comparison with similar ratio of other firms in the industry will reveal the comparative efficiency. So also the ratios for expenses of other head can be computed and compared on the same line expressed above.

Ratio analysis are subject to certain limitations. It is difficult to fix the basis for comparison. Ratios do not provide conclusive evidence of efficiency. Moreover ratios do not indicate future direction. They are only historical records of past events. Inspite of the limitations ratios provide a diagnostic role enabling deep insight into the marketing cost.

Limitations of Marketing Cost Analysis

Marketing cost analysis is subject to the following limitations.

1. Presence of joint costs

A major stumbling block with regard to marketing cost is the presence of joint costs. Marketing functions are performed for many products. Therefore segregation of cost and anlysing them are somewhat difficult.

2. Absence of adequate details

Absence of adequate cost detail is another problem. As compared to the production function, marketing function suffer more on this account. In view of this fact the accuracy of the marketing cost analysis is questioned.

3. Inaccessible data

Most data which are relevant to marketing cost analysis are outside the purview of a firm's marketing programme. Details pertaining to competitor's spending is an example thereby the comparative analysis is difficult and less meaningful.

4. Quantification of data

Marketing decision making is associated with information and details that cannot be so accurately quantified. The prospective buyers behaviour in the purchase decision process in one such qualitative aspect suffers from in accruable quantification. This sort of qualitative aspects also contribute towards marketing cost and that delimit the accuracy of cost analysis.

5. Inaccurate details

Efficient analysis of marketing cost depends on the accuracy of cost records and reports forwarded by all the functional heads involved in the performance of marketing activities. These functional heads depend in turn on their subordinates. The accuracy associated with these reports is vital to enable a meaningful and reliable cost analysis.

6. Lack of standardised cost

In view of the interaction of multiple uncontrollable variables, setting standard cost for different functional heads is difficult. Variance cannot be determined accurately which leads to the difficulty of measuring the cost effectiveness.

Marginal Costing in Relation to Marketing

Performance of marketing functions implies a number of decision making. Pertaining to important issues such as product planning and development, pricing, promotion strategy, etc. In the process of decision making the marketer resorts to various techniques and tools, one such is marginal costing.

Marginal costing is defined by The Institute of Cost And Management Accountant London as "It is the ascertainment of marginal cost and of the effect on profit of changes in the volume or type of output by differentiating between fixed and variable costs." The Institute adds that marginal costing is a technique by which only variable costs are charged to operations, processes of products leaving all indirect costs to be written off against profits in the period in which such costs arise. Obviously marginal costing is concerned with such of those direct costs which can be identified and assigned directly.

Also the institute defines marginal cost as "is the amount at any given volume of output by which aggregate costs are changed, if the volume of output is increased or decreased by one unit". The marginal cost concept confines to unit cost which refers to the cost created by the production of one additional unit. If A_1 and A_2 are the costs associated with the output level of B_1 and B_2 then A_1 - A_2 is the incremental cost and A_1 - A_2/B_1-B_2 stands as the marginal costs.

Marginal costing technique draws a clear distinction between fixed costs and variable costs. Fixed cost is a constant cost that are invariant with respect to changes in the output level. Generally fixed costs are likely to vary only in the long run and not during short run. Fixed costs depend mainly on effluxion of time and do not vary directly with volume or rate of output. Variable cost on the other hand vary in tune with the output. At the zero level of output the variable cost is also zero. Variable cost vary either proportionately or more or less proportionately. These are costs which are partly fixed and partly variable and they are termed as semivariable or semi fixed costs. The distinction between fixed, variable, semi fixed/variable costs assume significance in the light of the application of marginal costing as a technique for decision making.

The illustration presented below will explain the distinctions of marginal cost method from the total cost method.

Total Cost Method

	Period I Output (5000 units)	Period II Output (10000 units)	Period III Output (15000 units)
Direct material @ 45 per unit	25,000	50,000	75,000
Direct labour @ 3 per unit	15,000	30,000	45,000
	40,000	80,000	1,20,000
Over heads :			
Variable @Rs.2/unit	10,000	20,000	30,000
Fixed	20,000	20,000	20,000
Total cost	70,000	1,20,000	1,70,000
P/Loss	-10,000	Nil	+10,000
Sales @ 12 Rs.	60,000	1,20,000	1,80,000

Marginal Cost Method

	Period I	Period II	Period III
Direct material	25,000	50,000	75,000
Direct labour	15,000	30,000	45,000
Overhead - Variable	10,000	20,000	30,000
Marginal cost (B)	50,000	1,00,000	1,50,000
Contribution (A - B)	10,000	20,000	30,000
Sales (A)	60,000	1,20,000	1,80,000
Contribution	10,000	20,000	30,000
Fixed cost	20,000	20,000	20,000
	-10,000	Nil	10,000

Application of Marginal Costing in Marketing Related Decision Makings

The application of marginal costing technique in some of the key marketing decision areas is presented below under various heads.

1. Product Mix Decisions

Product mix as defined by Philip Kotler is a set of all product assessment inclusive of all product lines and items that a particular seller offer for sale to the buyer". Thus product mix is the total of all product items a seller offer for sale. Product mix of M/s.Procter and Gamble includes tooth paste, soap, detergent and so on. Product line on the other hand refers to product items that have related usage or satisfy same group of customer. The breadth as well as depth of product mix is associated with the number of product line as well as number of items concerned in the product mix.

Usually the product mix of a company consists of wider range of products for the following reasons.

- To compensate the position of the product items in different stages of product life cycle.
- To regulate fluctuating sales volume
- To have maximum utilization of resources available
- To distribute the production as well as marketing cost on a wider basis.

Marginal costing plays vital role in relation to product mix decision making.

Marketer will be confronted with changing product mix in view of any one or more of the following reasons.

- Changing demand conditions
- More Profitable use of available resources
- Technological changes
- Changing conditions of competition

Product mix is considered as best when it yields maximum contribution. Marginal costing technique enables to find out the contribution and thereby direct the marketer to opt for the best suited product mix under a given situation.

The following illustration explains the application of marginal costing in the decision pertaining to selection of best product mix.

A simulated cost situation of a company producing two products A and B is given below :

	Product	Per unit Rs.
Direct materials	A	10
Direct materials	B	9
Direct wages	A	3
Direct wages	B	2
Fixed expenses Rs.800		

Variable expenses are allotted to product as 100% of direct wages.

Sales price	A	20
Sales price	B	15

Product mix

1. 100 units of product A and 200 of B
2. 150 units of product A and 150 of B
3. 200 units of product A and 100 of B

In case of the above situation the marketer can resort to marginal costing technique and thereby arrive at contribution as detailed below :

	Product A Rs.	Product B Rs.
Direct materials	10	9
Direct wages	3	2
Variable expenses	3	2
	16	13
Contribution	4	2
Selling price	20	15

Case 1. 100 A + 200 B = (100 × 4) + (200 × 2)
= 800

2. 150 A + 150 B = (150 × 4) + (150 × 3)
= 900

3. 200 A + 100 B = (200 × 4) + (100 × 4)
= 1000

Contribution is maximum in case 3 i.e., Rs.1000. Deducting the fixed cost Rs.800 profit is Rs.200. Hence the marketer can arrive at a decision to opt for that type of a product mix consisting of 200 units of product A and 100 units of B.

2. Product : Drop or Add Decision

Drop or add decision is concerned with deleting an existing or introducing a new product item in the existing product line. It may also include introducing a new product line itself. Marketer has to take into account of various factors such as competition, technology, consumer behaviour, alternative use of available resources, profitability and so on. Among the various factors profitability assumes key place. A typical marketing situation is detailed below to explain how marginal costing is helpful to arrive at decision pertaining to dropping or adding a product item.

A company has three products viz., P1, P2 and P3. The past records show that P3 is continuously incurring loss. The estimated income statement is as below :

	P1	P2	P3	Total
Sales	5,00,000	4,00,000	1,00,000	10,00,000
Variable expenses	2,95,000	2,80,000	75,000	6,50,000
Contribution	2,05,000	1,20,000	25,000	3,50,000
Fixed expense	75,000	75,000	75,000	2,25,000
Operating expense	1,30,000	45,000	- 50,000	1,25,000

The supervisors salary included Rs.20,000. Marketer is considering to delete product P3. In this situation marginal costing technique will enable to arrive at a decision. The over all change in the profitability by deleting the product in question is worked out as below :

	With product P3	Without product P3
Sales	10,00,000	9,00,000
Variable expense	6,50,000	5,75,000
Fixed expenses	2,25,000	2,25,000
	4,25,000	3,50,000

The above details show that it would not be advisable to go for deletion of P3 in view of the reduction in the net margin.

4. Market Share Decision

Market share of a firm refers to that portion of the total demand which is been met by an individual firm. The firms market share is subject to expansion or contraction in tune with the nature of fluctuation of the factors so associated with the firm's product. Expanding or contracting the market share is a vital area of marketing decision making as there is every likelihood of changes in the profit margin. The additional contribution gained or lost assumes significance to decide on this matter. The following example illustrates the situation. The cost sheet of a product is given as under :

		Rs. P
Direct material		7.00
Direct wages		8.00
Factory overhead		
Fixed	1.00	
Variable	0.50	1.50
Administrative expenses		0.75
Selling and distribution		
Fixed	0.50	
Variable	0.25	0.75
		14.00

The selling price per unit is Rs. 15. The data pertaining to the output level of 50,000 units. The capacity of the firm is 65,000 units. There is a chance to expand the market by 15,000 units at a selling price of Rs.10 per unit.

The contribution by 15,000 units to be worked out as below :

		Rs.
Direct material		1,05,000
Direct wages		6,000
Prime cost		1,65,000
Factory over head		
Fixed	15,000	
Variable	7,500	

Administrative expense		22,500
Selling & distribution		11,250
Fixed	7,500	
Variable	3,750	
		11,250
		2,10,000
Sales		1,50,000
Contribution		60,000

Under the above situation the expansion of market share is a viable decision.

5. Pricing Decisions

Pricing decisions are so very important for the reasons that among other things, it is the price of the product that can influence the purchase decision of a prospective buyer. Under the normal circumstances the price will be based on full cost basis, but under certain conditions the marketer has to opt for prices which are just equal to the marginal cost. The marginal cost pricing method is followed under the following conditions :

* When the marketer introduces the product in the market
* When the product has to compete with well established brands
* When the product reaches its decline stage
* When the product is a defective product
* When entering the foreign market
* When the marketer wants to dispose the surplus stock.

Under the said circumstances the price is arrived taking into account of the contribution generated by the product. The following illustration specify how marginal costing helps in fixation of prices.

	Rs.	Rs.
Sales (40,000 units)		3,60,000
Direct materials	1,20,000	
Direct labour	80,000	

Variable overhead	40,000	
Fixed overhead	1,00,000	
		3,40,000
		20,000

It is proposed to reduce the selling price from Rs. 9 to Rs. 8 per unit. It is anticipated that if reduction in the price is made, the volume of sales will increase by 30,000 unit.

In the above circumstance, in order to reach suitable decision marginal costing will be useful as under. The marketer has to take into account of the contribution generated by the proposed change in the price. The contribution is calculated as under.

		At 40000 units Rs.	At 70000 units Rs.
Sales		3,60,000	5,60,000
Less :	Marginal cost		
	Material	1,20,000	2,10,000
	Labour	80,000	1,40,000
	Variable overhead	40,000	70,000
		1,20,000	1,40,000
Less :	Fixed cost	1,00,000	1,00,000
		20,000	40,000

The working above reveals that a reduction in the price level increases the contribution by 80,000. Hence the price reduction is a rational decision. Similarly on the other circumstances too the contribution is to be calculated and accordingly the changes in price decision can be effectively arrived at.

6. Extension or Suspension of Distribution Outlets

The marketer may have a number of distribution outlets depending upon the nature of product, nature of consumer and so on. Decision pertaining to continuation or suspension of distribution outlet often arise in view of the changing market conditions. Under these circumstances marginal costing enables a marketer to arrive at appropriate decisions.

The following situation illustrate the usefulness of marginal costing on the above circumstances.

A company has three distribution outlets D1, D2 and D3. The cost details pertaining to be three departments are as below:

	D1 Rs.	D2 Rs.	D3 Rs.
Sales	80,000	40,000	60,000
Marginal costs			
Direct material	10,000	5,000	10,000
Labour	4,000	5,000	16,000
Variable overhead	10,000	5,000	20,000
Fixed overhead	20,000	10,000	20,000
Total cost	44,000	25,000	66,000

The management is interested in closing down D3. Under these circumstances the contribution by the three departments, also contribution by the two departments (in case D3 is close down) are to be calculated as under :

	D1 Rs.	D2 Rs.	D3 Rs.
Sales	80,000	40,000	60,000
Less			
Direct material	10,000	5,000	10,000
Direct labour	4,000	5,000	16,000
Variable overhead	10,000	5,000	20,000
Contribution	56,000	25,000	14,000
Total contribution	95,000		
Less : Total cost	50,000		
	45,000		

In case D3 is discontinued the position will be :

		D1	D2
Sales		80,000	40,000
Less : Marginal cost			
Direct material		10,000	5,000
Direct labour		4,000	5,000
Variable overhead		10,000	5,000
		56,000	25,000
Total contribution	81,000		
Less : Fixed cost	50,000		
Profit	31,000		

It is obvious that from the viewpoint of profit it has reduced to 31,000 from 45,000. Therefore it would be a wise decision to continue D3 rather than closing down.

7. Strategic Factors

Strategic factors refer to key factors or limiting factors that determine the operational viability. Decisions on the strategic factors deserve considerable attention. Strategic factors may be material, labour, equipment, time, demand etc. Key factor is also subject to change from time to time as well as from one operation to the other.

The under mentioned illustration show how strategic factor affects relative profitability and thereby influence the decision.

The particulars pertaining to products P1 and P2 are as below :

	Per unit	
	P1	P2
Sales	100 Rs.	120 Rs.
Material required	2 Kg.	3 Kg.
Material cost	10 Rs.	15 Rs.
Direct wages	15 Rs.	10 Rs.
Direct expenses	5 Rs.	6 Rs.
Machine hours	3	2
Overhead expenses		
Fixed	5	10
Variable	15	20

Direct wages per hour is Rs. 5

Under the above situation assuming that the raw material as the strategic factor, availability of which is 10,000 kg and maximum sales potential of each product being 3500 units. The product mix that will yield maximum profit will be arrived at as below.

		P1		P2
Sales		100		120
Less : Material	10		15	
Wages	15		10	
Direct expenses	5		6	
Variable overhead	15		20	
		45		51
Contribution		55.0		69.0
Contribution per kg of material		27.5		23.0
Contribution per machine hour		18.3		34.5

When raw material is scarce and limited to 10,000 kgs and maximum production limits is 3,500 units of each the material allotment would be

Product P1 - 7000 kgs for 3500 units
Product P2 - 3000 kgs for 1000 units

Total contribution	= 3500 × Rs.55 + 1000 × 69
	= 2,61,500
Total fixed cost	= 3500 × 5 + 1000 × 10
	= 27,500
Total profit	= Total contribution - Total fixed cost
	= 2,61,500 – 27,500
	= 2,34,000

Thus when there is a key factor the marginal costing enable to arrive at appropriate decision.

8. Profitability Level Decisions

Maintaining a desired level of profitability is another critical decision making area which is assisted by marginal costing. The volume of sales needed to have a desired level of profit can be ascertained by means of marginal costing. An example is presented below to explain the situation.

A company produces and markets a highly competitive product. The company proposes to reduce the selling price, but the present level of profit should be maintained. The proposed reduction in selling price might be 5%, 10% or 15%. The other details available are

Present sales Turnover(30,000)		3,00,000
Variable cost (3,00,000 units)	1,80,000	
Fixed cost	70,000	
		2,50,000
Net profit		50,000

Present selling price is Rs. 10.

The company is provided with the following options.

a. Price reduction by 5%, then price will be Rs. 9.50
b. Price reduction by 10%, then price will be Rs. 9
c. Price reduction by 15%, then price will be Rs. 8.50

Contribution at various proposed selling prices

	Price reduction		
	5%	10%	15%
Selling price	9.50	9.00	8.50
Variable cost	6.00	6.00	6.00
	3.50	3.00	2.50

Total contribution required to maintain the present level of profit can be worked out as below

	Rs.
Fixed expenses	70,000
Profit as present	50,000
	1,20,000

Units to be sold to earn the total contribution of Rs. 1,20,000 to maintain the present level of profit.

a. At a price reduced by 5% 1,20,000/3.50 = 34,286 units
b. If price is reduced by 10% 1,20,000/3.00 = 40,000 units
c. If price is reduced by 15% 1,20,000/2.50 = 48,000 units

On the above line marginal costing enables to maintain desired level of profit, even if the circumstances necessitates changes in price of the product.

Marketing decisions are bound by various considerations which are related to market conditions, consumer attitude, resource availability and so on. In this context arriving at marketing decisions purely based on cost consideration alone would never be an absolutely appropriate approach. Moreover marketer has to encounter with the problem of segregation of cost into fixed as well as variable which offers the base for marginal costing technique to operate. Marketing decisions are concerned with longer perspective but marketing costing focus more on short run benefits. On these lines marketer has to play safely when using marginal costing as a decision making tool.

Cost Volume Profit Decisions

Decisions pertaining to cost-volume and profit relationship are vital for marketing the product as they influence the operation as well as the efficiency of marketing functions. The interrelationship between cost-volume and profit makes marketing decisions more complex and challenging, but under conditions of uncertainty the cost-volume-profit relationship helps to arrive at appropriate decisions. Some situations are presented below :

* That the profit plan envisage volume and cost alternatives.
* What will be the fluctuation in the rate of profit if the sales volume flucatuate ?
* What rate of change in the production cost significantly affect profit rate ?
* What is the additional sales volume required, to meet increasing production cost ?
* Which product item, salesman, sales territory contribute most to the profit ?
* Drop or add a product item in the product line.
* Impact of changes in selling price.

The cost-volume-profit relationship analysis assist to arrive at meaningful decisions on issues listed above.

Break Even Analysis

Break even analysis reveals the relationship between the volume and cost of production on the one hand and the revenue and profit obtained from the sales on the other. The captured relation of fixed cost, variable cost, value of output, sales price etc., to the company under consideration. Break even sales volume is defined as the sales volume at which the sales revenue is equal to the total cost. The break even volume may be defined in terms of units of turnover or in terms of sales value of units sold. In a nut shell break even volume is that volume at which revenue is sufficient to cover both variable cost and fixed cost for the financial period under consideration.

Break Even Point

Break even point is that point of activity where the total revenue and total expenses are equal. It is the point of zero profit where losses cease to occur while profit have not yet begun. In case the firm produces and sells less than the suggested by break even point the firm would incur loss. If the firm produces and sells more than the level given by break even point it makes profit. Therefore the break even point is the indicator of profitable level of marketing operation. The break even point can be arrived at, by preparing break even chart.

Break Even Chart

Break even chart visualizes the profit or loss implications at different levels of sales. It is an analysis in graphics form of production, sales and profit. A typical break even chart is shown in Exh. VIII.

In the chart 'OX' represent the volume of production, 'OP' is the amount of production, 'OQYX' represents the fixed cost, 'QZY' represents variable cost, 'TR' represent total revenue line, 'TC' represent total cost line and 'BEP' is the break even point.

The break even point may be computed in terms of units of products are in terms of total volume of sales. Break even volume in units may be stated as

$$\text{Break even volume} = \frac{\text{Total fixed cost}}{\text{Contribution unit}}$$

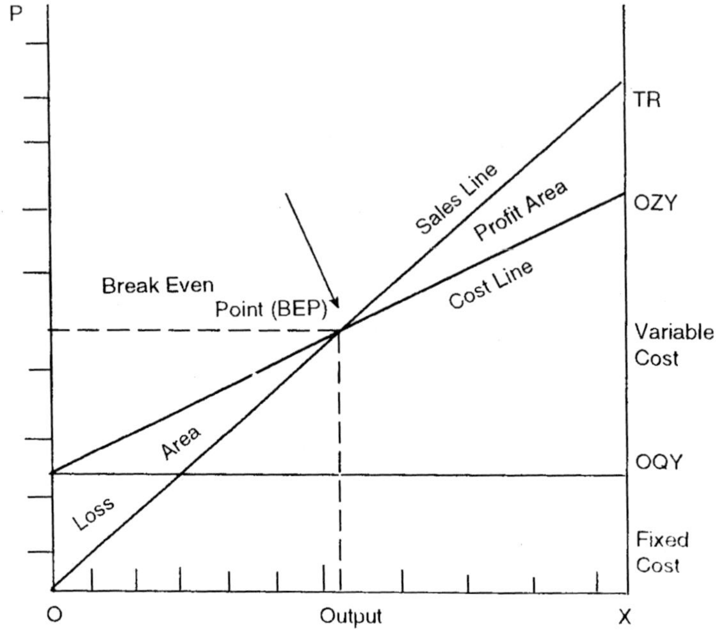

Exhibit VIII: Break Even Chart

Assume that the business firm produces a single product the selling price is Rs.10 per unit and variable cost Rs.6 per unit, the firms fixed cost annually is 1,60,000. The break even volume can be computed as below.

Break even volume = 1,60,000/4 = 4

The firm has to sell 40,000 units annually for the firm to be at the profit or no loss state.

Usually one can express Break even point in three ways.

1. as a number of units of goods sold.
2. as a volume of sales.
3. as a percentage of plant capacity.

The following example illustrates the calculation of BEP on the above three ways.

A coastal ship can carry maximum 1,00,000 passengers per month at a fair of Rs. 850. Variable cost is Rs.100/- while fixed cost is 7,50,000 per month.

1. Break even quality

$$= \frac{\text{Total fixed cost}}{\text{Price per unit} - \text{variable cost}}$$

$$= \frac{7{,}50{,}000}{850 - 100} = 1{,}00{,}000 \text{ passengers}$$

2. Break even sales

$$= \frac{\text{Total fixed cost}}{1 - \text{variable cost / price}}$$

$$= \frac{7{,}50{,}000}{1 - 100/850} = 85{,}00{,}000$$

3. Break even percentage of capacity :

$$= \frac{\text{Total fixed cost}}{\text{Price} - (\text{Average variable cost})} \times 100$$

$$= \frac{7{,}50{,}000}{(850 - 100) \times 1{,}00{,}000} \times 100$$

$$= 10\%$$

The findings on each of the three cases are uniform inspite of the different approach adopted.

Margin of Safety

The excess of budgeted sales of product over the break even is generally known as margin of safety. It may be expressed as below

$$\text{Margin of safety} = \frac{\text{Sales at BEP}}{\text{Sales}} \times 100$$

The margin of safety is an approximation since its validity depends upon the accuracy of cost estimates at the break even point.

The break even analysis is subject to various limitations.

Some of them are

* It assumes constant relationship between output to cost.
* Non inclusion of changes in products selling price impart unrealism.
* Various other factors such as technological improvement, managerial effectiveness are not included.

Inspite of the limitations, in view of the simplicity and understandability the break even point is widely used by marketing decision makers.

5

Marketing Cost Control : Technique and Tools

The performance of marketing activity is to be reviewed and controlled towards the desired marketing goals. Marketing cost control involves analyses of various marketing activities such as sales volume, distribution cost, market share, customer satisfaction and so on.

The sales volume analysis is concerned with evaluating the difference between actual sales and the sales goals. The variation is to be found and the reasons for such variation is to be probed into. There may be a number of reasons for decline or increase in the volume of sales.The major reason found is to be subjected to micro sales analysis which will pin point the exact reason for the difference in the sales volume, accordingly corrective actions are to be initiated.

With respect to distribution cost analysis the distribution cost is to be divided under two heads—direct and indirect. Direct distribution cost refer to costs whose application to specific segments of market are readily ascertainable. Indirect distribution cost are those which are incurred for more than one segment of market and therefore cannot be traced directly to specific product or customer. Distribution cost may also be classified as to fixed and variable in terms of its subjective change with the volume of production. While fixed distribution cost remain unchanged variable distribution cost either proportionately or absolutely changes in accordance with the sales volume. A classified distribution cost analysis will enable to determine channel efficiency.

Market share analysis refers to the analysis pertaining to the share of total demand which is being met by the organization under consideration. Thus this analysis will reveal the organizations over all market share in relation to its competitors.

This analysis will enable to find out the organizations position in the industry.

Customer satisfaction analysis will enable to find out the extent of customer satisfaction with respect to the products and services offered. It takes into account the number of complaints received from the customers, types of such complaints and so on.

Tools to Control Market Activities

Budgeting

Marketing functions are performed under conditions of uncertainty caused mostly by the influence of external factors. In the process of performing marketing functions, marketer invariably assumes risks. Risk is unavoidable, but minimizing risk is possible with the help of carefully planned approach. There are many managerial tools, that are available which enable planning, regulating and controlling marketing activities. Budgeting is one of the managerial tools available that assist to perform marketing activities effectively towards the desired marketing objectives.

Budget is defined by the terminology of cost accountancy as "a financial and/or quantitative statement prepared and approved prior to a defined period of time policy to be pursued during that period for the purpose of attaining a given objective". Budget differ from forecast in the sense that forecast precedes the preparation of budget it relates the probable events whereas budget is based on the implication of a forecast. Budget is thus a blue print of a protective plan of action of a definite period of time. It presents the plans objectives and policies in numerical terms.

Budgetary control is the process of determining various budgeted figures for the enterprise for the future period and thus comparing the budgeted figures with the actual performance for calculating variance if any. According to Brown and Howard "Budgeting control is a system of controlling costs which include the preparation of budgets, coordinating the department and establishing responsibilities, comparing actual performance with budgeted and acting upon results to achieve maximum profitability". Thus budgetary control is the process of implementing the budget and controlling the activities towards the desired, predetermined direction.

* Classification as per functions :
  - Sales budget
  - Production budget
  - Purchase budget
  - Cash budget
  - Finance budget
* Classification as per time
  - Long term budget
  - Short term budget
  - Current budget
* Classification on the basis of flexibility
  - Fixed budget
  - Flexible budget

As regards the marketing activities the budget can be broadly classified under the following heads :

Product Line Based Marketing Budget

A firm whose product mix consist of two or more lines of product, the budget can be prepared by taking into account of the specific requirements of each product line. Assuming that, a firms product mix comprises of two lines of which one is cosmetics and other is home appliances. The budgets can be of the following types :

Budget Related to Cosmetics

1. Production budget
   - Material budget
   - Labour budget
   - Direct expenses budget
2. Sales budget
3. Advertisement budget
4. Distribution budget
5. Sales personnel budget
6. Market finance budget

In the same line above budgets related to home appliances can also be formed. This sort of classified form of budget preparation enable marketer to allocate available resources depending on requirement of each product item. The actual performance can be monitored from the viewpoint to measure the variance between the projected and factual expense thereby help to ascertain the viability of holding the product item in the line.

Function Based Marketing Budget

Function based marketing budget focus attention on planning and allocation of resources taking into account of the specific functional requirement. Function based marketing budget include the following :

- Production budget
- Purchase budget
- Storage and warehousing budget
- Sales promotion budget
- Distribution budget
- Sales force budget
- Finance budget

Production Budget

Production budget is closely associated with production functions rather than marketing. However the Production budget is a quantitative expression of the estimated volume of production. This budget is prepared after taking into consideration of the estimated opening stock estimated sales and the desired closing stock of each, item of product concerned. Also the other factors taken into account in the preparation of production budget are the time lag between production and sales. Sales programme, material, labour, plant availability, market conditions length of production cycle, length of time required to secure inputs etc.

A thorough idea about production budget and coordination of production budget with that of sales budget enable smooth marketing operation. Marketers normally fixes the sales target for one year period. Fixation of such target not taking into account of the production budget will either lead to deficit or surplus production as the case it may be. The illustration of material cost budget, labour cost budget, and other direct cost budget and production budget is shown in Exh. IX.

Sales Budget

Ultimately the marketer wants to achieve as much sales as possible in a given market condition. The performance of marketing function is directed towards attaining more and more sales volume only. As such sales budget assumes importance. Sales budget essentially presupposes sales forecast. There are many methods of sales forecast. They include

1. Executive committee opinion method
2. Sales for composite method
3. Correlation analysis method
4. Trend and cycle analysis method
5. Multiple approach method

The executive committee method involves pooling of the views of several top level marketing executives and other functional heads and thereby forecast the sales. Under the sales force composite method, the salesmen are expected to estimate probable sales in their territory for a given period of time. This method has the advantage of reliability, because it starts with the individuals who are close and best acquainted with the customers. Correlation analysis, trend and cycle analysis, and multiple approach method are common statistic methods employed to provide greater accuracy in sales forecasting by eliminating personal opinion. The selection of a particular method depends on specific requirement of the marketer in relation to resource available and the application of sales forecast. Sales budget may be prepared showing budgeted sales under anyone or combination of the following heads.

Product Item

If a firm's product mix consist of a number of product items, the sales budget can be prepared with reference to each product item.

Exhibit IX: Input Budget

Product Input Cost	*Jan.*	*Feb.*	*Mar.*	*Apr.*	*May*	*June*
Item A MC LC ODC IDC	*Unit=*	*Unit=*	*Unit =*	*Unit=*	*Unit=*	*Unit=*
Total						
Item B MC LC ODC IDC						
Total						

Market Segment

Under this method the heterogeneous market is divided into homogeneous segments on some selected basis such as demographic profile or geographic profile of the buyers in the market. The budget is prepared with reference to each segment. Sales budget pertaining to North zone, South zone, East zone and West zone of India is an example of geographically segmented market based budget.

Sales Person

This budget is fixed taking into account the specific amount of sales that could be effected by each sales person concerned.

Time Period

Sales budget prepared in accordance to the time period namely weekly, monthly, quarterly or annual etc.

In most cases the sales budget will be a combination of different basis detailed above. Such a proforma sales budget is presented below.

Sales Budget

Segment	Product	Budget Quantity Rs.	Current sales Quantity Rs.	Deviation
	A			
North zone	B			
	C			
	D			
	A			
South zone	B			
	C			
	D			
	A			
East zone	B			
	C			
	D			
	A			
West zone	B			
	C			
	D			
Total				

Distribution Cost Budget

The distribution cost refers to the cost incurred in making the goods flow from the production centre to that of consumption centre. The distribution cost may be classified in terms of those marketing functions associated with ultimate distribution of the product to the consumer. Distribution budget is concerned with determining the cost of distribution function, establishing units of measurement of the functional services, development of standard cost for such services and using such standards for cost control process. Distribution cost may also be classified under two heads or direct as well as indirect. Direct costs are those which are immediately identifiable with specific functions and there is no problem of allocation. Indirect distribution cost are those which are identified with the entire company or entire marketing activity. Such cost are to be allocated on suitable basis. Certain costs are neither certainly direct nor indirect. They are semi direct costs. The essential steps involved in the distribution cost budget are as below.

1. Determination of direct as well as indirect distribution cost.
2. Determination of basis of allocation costs which are fixed as well as variable.
3. Budgetary distribution cost to analyze costs which are fixed as well as variable.
4. Estimating the amount of distribution costs in accordance with estimated sales.
5. Preparation of estimates for the submission for the budget period.

A proforma of selling and distribution budget is presented below :

Distribution Budget Cost

Item	Jan	Feb	March	April
* Cost of Demand Creation				
Salesmen salary				
Commission				
Travelling expenses				
* Cost of Handling Orders				
Storage				
Packing				
Billing				
* Cost of Credit Collection				
Interest				
Travelling expenses				
Stationary				
* General				

Sales Promotion Budget

In view of the significance of the sales promotion efforts sales promotion measures are to be budgeted separately. Sales promotion measures usually consists of advertisement, publicity, personal selling and other promotion measures. Among these Marketers' attention is more with respect to advertisements as such sales promotion budgets focus more attention on advertisement and the promotion budget may be termed as advertisement budget also. Allocation to advertisement budget takes into account, factors such as

* Size of market
* Competition
* Frequency of advertisement
* Product nature
* Financial position and the like

For the matter of allocating advertisement budget one has to take into account the relative influence of advertisement in the volume of sales. Three hypothetical situations are possible. They are

1. No Carry Over Situation

Under the situation irrespective of the budgeted allocation on advertisement, the volume of sales will be the same.

2. High/Medium Carry Over Situation

Under this situation there will be more than proportionate volume of sales as compared to the increased effected in the budgeted allocation for advertisements.

3. Low Carry Over Situation

Under this situation there will be less than proportionate volume of sales as compared to the increase effected in the budgeted allocation for advertisement.

An optimum allocation to advertising budget is therefore necessary. The optimal advertisement budget strategy suggested by Eugne J Kelly and William Lazer is as below.

The effect of competitive advertising on a brands optimal advertising depends on the relative strength of the brand appeal in terms of its attributes. If all competitors are equal then the advertisement budget in terms of number of competitions (N) the industry price (NP) and advertising elasticity (no) the share of marked price elasticity of brands, the cost of manufacturing and distribution of the product, and the probability (bpda) of consumers brand choice being influenced in part by advertising.

$$\text{Price/Unit} = \frac{\text{Cost/Unit } np + e\,(N-1)}{n + e\,(N-1) - N}$$

and

$$\text{Sales promotional expense/unit} = \frac{\text{Cost/unit bpda } (N-1)}{np + e\,(N-1) - N}$$

That is when all other factors being held constant

$$D(P,a) = D[P_o\, a_o] \frac{[P]^{-np}}{[P_o]} \frac{[a]^{na}}{[a_o]}$$

Where D(P,a) = industry demand at price P and advertising level a, where industry price is weighted average price of all brands in the market, each brands contribution being weighted with respect to its share of market and D(Po,Ao) = industry demand at some base price level Po and base advertising level.

In view of the resource, crunch and other related reasons, the method of allocation to advertisement budget assumes importance, usually the basis of advertisement budget is as below :

* All you can afford
* Percentage on sales
* Firms objectives
* Competitors allocation

Usually the advertisement budget suffers from the problem that the cost benefit effectiveness cannot easily be estimated. The firm lag between the occurrence of expenditure and the effect of varying media influence. The proforma of advertisement budget and sales promotion budget are presented below :

Advertising Budget

Media/Quarter	Jan-Mar	Apr-June	July-Sep	Oct-Dec
Print				
Broadcast				
Telecast				
Others				

Sales Promotion Budget

Promoters/period	Jan-Mar	Apr-June	July-Sep	Oct-Dec
Method				
Advertisement				
Publicity				
Personal Selling				
Other Promotion				
Total				

Marketing Research and Development Budget

Marketing research and development activity is one of the vital marketing activities. In order to probe into the future changes marketing research and development activity is to be carried out continuously. Budget allocation to market research and development assumes significance.

The allocation to the research and development depends upon the nature of the company, product, Competition extent of involvement in research and development activity and the like factors.

Marketing research and development budget is usually an appropriation budget. Marketing research executives confine and apportion the financial commitment with respect to Marketing Research and Development within the total financial outlay allocated to research and development. The usual problem with respect to the operation of marketing research and development budget as below :

* Research and development is associated with many intangible activities therefore it is very difficult to predict the financial requirement.

* For the same reason above, it is very difficult to predict the extent of utilization of fund allocated to marketing research and development.
* Research and development is more technical area predicting the financial requirement in addition to knowledge pertaining to marketing aspects.

Marketing Research and Development Budget

Activity	Jan-Mar	Apr-June	July-Sep	Oct-Dec
Marketing research Activity (A1)				
Marketing research Activity (A2)				
Marketing research Activity A3				

Marketing Performance Budget

Marketing performance budget is defined by National Institute of Bank Management as "a process of anlysing identifying simplifying and crystallizing specific performance activities of a job to be achieved over a period of time within the framework of orgasnisational objectives". Thus performance budget aim towards achievement of specific goal over a period of time. The preparation of marketing performance budget is with the chief of marketing department.

As regards the performance budget it has to focus attention on aspects such as market share, product development — distribution advertisement campaign profitability and the like.

The aspects identified are simplified and crystallized in view of the main goal of marketing activities. Performance expected is budgeted in tune with each aspect and result is compared and variations will be dealt accordingly.

Marketing Performance Budget : Marketing Department

Identified Performance area	Budgeted				Actual	Variance
	J-M	A-J	J-A	S-D		
Market Share :						
National						
International						
Product						
New addition of item						
Deletion						
New lines						
Advertisement						
Campaigns						
Media Coverage						
Press						
Broadcast						
Telecast						
Other						
Distribution :						
Whole sale advertisement						
Retail Outlet volume						
Marketing Research and Development						
New Product						

Marketing Personnel : Salesmen
Marketing Performance Budget : Marketing Executives
Identified Performance Budgeted Actual Variance area
Product Development Sales Quota
Sales travels
Market Programme
Development of sales price
Market opportunity
Marketing Cost

The problem pertaining to performance budget are manifold in the sense that some performance area cannot be accurately quantified. Also performance cannot be confind to a particular accounting period or budget period leading estimating the variance and corrective action thereafter.

Marketing Finance Budget

The objectives of marketing finance budget is to estimate the financial requirements to perform the marketing operations to determine the source and amount that can be obtained and also to coordinate with the company's total financial planning.

Sales

Application of Finance

On Advertisement
On Travel
On Commission
On Research and Development

Zero Base Marketing Budget

The technique zero base budgeting is now been very popularly adopted. In contrast to the traditional budget in the zero base budget, no reference is made to the previous years budgeted allocation and other relevant details. As such zero base budgeting is not a repeated exercise of previous years budget with suitable additions and deduction. It is a budget started from the zero base.

As regards zero base budgeting in marketing, the marketing manager is expected to make the entire marketing activity into a number of smaller decision of making units. Without any regard to master budget's increase or decrease, the marketing executive fix the budgetary requirement for each decision making unit, and the marketing manager has to justify the rationality behind opting for budgeted amount.

The major decision units under budgeting marketing area are those of

- Product related
- Promotion related and
- Place (Distribution) related

Each decision units are to be further divided into sub decisions units as amenable for fund allocation, administration and appraisal. The major product related decision units are the new product development packaging, product launching, product diversification, modification etc. The major promotion relationed sub decision units are advertisement, publicity, salesmanship other promotional activities. Each subdivision may include further subdivisions also. Similarly place related decision units incorporate whole sales, retail, distribution showrooms etc. The marketing executive in coordination with the respective functional heads give budget requirement from the base or zero without reference to previous budget period. The proforma of zero base marketing budget is as shown below :

Zero Base Marketing Budget

Decision units	Sub decision units	Budget J - M	A - J	J - S	O - D
Product related	New product				
	Product modification				
	Product launching				
	Product diversification				

Promotion Advertisement related

* Press]
* Radio
* TV
* Other sales force

1. Training
2. Remuneration
3. Commission other methods
1. Direct mail
2. Vehicular advertisement
3. Compliments

4. Free gifts
   Place related Wholesale
   Retail
   Outlets
   Commission

The marketing executive has to justify the proposed allotment on the following lines.

* Necessity of such amount
* Competition
* Economic benefit
* Risk involved of the amount is not allotted and so on.

From the marketers viewpoint zero base budgeting is innovative and most appropriate, in view of the consistently changing marketing environment and the risk associated thereby. The changing environment is to be viewed afresh rather than considering the situation merely an extension of past events. So also the budget allotment.

Marketing Responsibility Accounting

The competitive nature of marketing functions essentially invite higher responsibility on the part of the marketing functionaries. Responsibility stands for the accountability of one's action. Being responsible implies being accountable. As regards the marketing function, the effective performance depends on the collective responsibility of each functionaries, associated with the marketing process right from need identification to need fulfilment.

Responsibility accounting is been defined as a system of accounting in which all costs and incomes both anticipated and actual are allocated to responsible managers. It differs from the traditional accounting pattern in the sense that in the traditional accounting all costs are to be allocated to manufacturing department and sections.

The method has the technical difficulty also. It divides the responsibility of those managers who are not concerned with the production function. However under responsibility accounting the cost of both budgeted as well as actual are allocated directly to those managers who are responsible for creating and discharging such expenses. For example with respect to expense of research and development it will be allocated first to the research and development chief executive in charge of that function. The expenditure will then be subdivided among other executives who reports to that chief executive. The process continues by further analysis and the allocation to whatever depth of detail is required. Thus as expressed by Robert Antony "Responsibility accounting is that type of management accounting that collect and reports both planned and actual information in terms of responsibility centres".

The Process of Responsibility Accounting

The process of responsibility accounting starts with fixation of the responsibility centres. Responsibility centre may be fixed by taking into any one of the prime basis like.

(a) Function (b) Products (c) Customers and so on. The distinguishing characteristics of the responsibility accounting is that to allocate the expenses to the executives incharge of the responsibility centres in such a way that the expenses fluctuate in tune with their decisions pertaining to that responsibility centre.

As regards marketing the responsibility centres identified are presented below. The responsibility centre is based on functional significance.

Function/Functional Head	Responsibility
Product development/product planning and development manager	Product research Product design Product package Branding
Sales promotion/ Sales promotion executive	* Advertisement companies decision * Media selection * Agency selection * Publicity * Personal selling * Appointment of salesmen training * Trade /exhibition

Distribution/Distribution Manager

* Storage
* Showrooms
* Wholesale distribution
* Retail distribution
* Quota fixation
* Transportation
* Commission

Price fixation

* Pricing
* Discount
* Markup
* Mark down

Marketing research

* Forecasting
* Consumer attitude
* Competition
* Government policy
* Technology

Market control

* Budgeting
* Auditing
* Portfolio analysis

The responsibility centre identified has a pyramiding impact i.e., at the lowest level the cost is controlled. It will have the impact up to the top most level of management.

The Pyramid Effect of Responsibility

The above exhibit explains the level of responsibility inter linkage at various hierarchy level.

Salesman (S1) from the Territory (T1) is responsible to the allotment of Rs.200/- towards his commission and travel expenditure. This responsibility level reflects in the responsibility level of the regional sales manager (RSM) who is incharge of Region 1 which consists of three territories so the responsibility level to be in the line of Rs.700/-. This further reflects in the responsibility of marketing manager (MM) who is incharge of three regions and the marketing managers responsibility level is by Rs.2500/-. Further this level reflects the overall responsibility level of the chief executive in charge of various functions and his responsibility level reaches to Rs.7500/-.

The task of isolation of expenses and changing responsibility centre is difficult in view of collective nature of performance. Also the cash incurred are the nature of controllable as well as uncontrollable. As such the functional heads have very little role to determine their fluctuation.

Marketing Profitability Accounting

Marketing profitability denotes the profit earned in view of the performance of marketing activity for a given period under consideration. Profitability accounting reveals the efficiency of the marketing activity performed.

Marketing profitability determination implies the following steps :

1. Allotment of Functional Expenses

The functional expenses are to be allotted to each activity concerned. For example a company reports that the administrative expenses is Rs.10,000. The marketer has to identify out of Rs.10,000 the amount applicable to marketing related functions. Assume that it is Rs.3000. The next step is this Rs.3000 is to be distributed in accordance to the nature of markrting activity. It may go as below :

Sales persons salary	1000
Packaging	300
Transport	300
Storage rent	50
Distribution	700
Advertising	200
Research	200
Stationery	250
Total	3000

This sort of allotment enables to attribute the expense to various marketing activity.

2. Segregation of Allotment Functional Expenses

The expense allotted above are to be further segregated on each marketing events. For e.g. advertising above i.e., Rs.200, that is to be segregated further as below :

Press	50
Radio	50
T.V.	100
	200

Also in tune with the number of ad. campaign it can be further distribuited
For each campaign cost 50/5 = Rs.10
Radio 5 campaign 50/5 = Rs.10
In TV two campaigns cost 100/2 = Rs.50

Similarly expenses can be deeply segregated.

3 Preparation of Accounting Statement for Marketing function

The Accounting Statements mainly constitute preparation of Profit and Loss A/c. Preparation can take place on any one of the basis

(1) Products basis
(2) Channel basis
(3) Customer basis
(4) Matrix basis

Taking a hyhpothetical situation of a company whose product mix consist of ice creams and cool drinks present its profit and loss statement as below :

(1) Product : ICE CREAM
Profit and Loss Statement

Item	Rs.	Rs.
Sales	xxxx	
Less Cost of Production	xxxx	xxxx
Gross Margin		

(contd...)

Item	Rs.	Rs.
Less Functional expenses		
Advertising	xx	
Distribution	xx	
Salesman	xx	
Showroom rent	xx	
Package	xx	
Transport	xx	
Plates	xx	
Straws	xx	
Depreciation	xx	xxx
Net Margin		xxxx

The same procedure is to be repeated in case of cool drink also. The net margin arrived in case of ice cream and cool drink clubbed together will give the total Net Margin.

(2) Channel basis : Product Ice Cream

The Channel based profit and loss statement will appear as below assume that the said firm has three channels.

Channel A : Direct retail outlet
B : Agents sales outlet
C : Retailers sales outlet

Channel

Item	A	B	C	Total
Sales	xx	xx	xx	xxxx
Less Cost of goods sold	xx	xx	xx	xxx
	xx	xx	xx	xxxx
Less Functional expenses :				
Advertisement				
Distribution				
Salesman				
Showroom rent				

Package				
Transport				
Plates				
Straws				
Depreciation	xx	xx	xx	xxx
	xx	xx	xx	xxxx

So also the channel based profit and loss statement can also be prepared. The same procedure to be repeated in the case of cool drinks.

3. Customer Basis — Ice Cream

Assuming that the firm has three types of customer segments.

Segment C1 : Individuals
Segment C2 : Functions/parties/group orders
Segment C3 : Institutions
The profit and loss statement will appear as below

	Segment			
Item	C1	C2	C3	Total
Sales	xx	xx	xx	xxx
Less : Cost of goods Sold	xx	xx	xx	xx
	xx	xx	xx	xxx
Less : Functional expenses				
Advertisement				
Distribution				
Salesman				
Showroom rent				
Package				
Transport				
Plates				
Straws				
Depreciation	xx	xx	xx	xxx
Net Margin	xx	xx	xx	xxx

Similar statement can be prepared for cold drinks also.

Marketing Audit

Marketing audit is a periodic examination of the marketing activities performed and the effectiveness associated with such performance. The need for reviewing and overhauling marketing functions is necessary to maintain and ensure greater efficiency in the performance of marketing activities. Even though methodological sophistication with respect to marketing audit is yet to be reached the need for implementing marketing audit is generally on the increase.

Marketing audit can be classified under two major heads viz., Horizontal marketing audit and vertical marketing audit. A horizontal marketing audit is more comprehensive that deal with marketing environment, competitors, Government attitude, market share and so on. Vertical marketing on the other hand, is more indepth audit thus is undertaken when the management wants to examine particular marketing activity in detail like sale force audit, advertisement audit and the like. Considering both types of marketing audit and also the purpose behind such audit the definition putforth by Philip Kotler et al runs as follows "A marketing audit is a comprehensive, systematic, independent and periodic examination of a company's or business unit's marketing environment, objectives, strategies and activities with the view of determining problem areas and opportunity and recommending a plan of action to improve the company's marketing performance".

The purpose of marketing audit is to evaluate how effectively the organization concerned is performing its marketing operations in terms of its strength, weakness, opportunities and threats associated with such organization. Marketing audit programme is both qualitative and quantitative in its characteristics.

The other important characteristics are as below :

1. Elaborate

The marketing audit is usually elaborate and not partial audit. It is possible that financial audit may be partial audit or elaborate audit. But in view of the interconnected nature of the marketing functions usually marketing audit is much elaborate audit only covering all aspects of marketing functions.

2. Continuous

Marketing audit is continuous in the sense that the marketing auditor's staff are continuously engaged in checking comparing and reporting details pertaining to marketing activities.

3. Optional

There is no statutory compulsion behind holding marketing audit. The organization on their own accord will come forward to adopt marketing audit in view of the specific merits associated therewith.

4. Internal

Marketing audit to a greater extent is performed internally by the staff of the organization concerned.

*** Objectives of Marketing Audit**

The objectives of marketing audit is listed below :
1. To study and evaluate the adequacy and effectiveness of the performance of marketing activities.
2. To ascertain the extent of compliance of the practice of marketing activities with that of the predetermined marketing policies plans and procedure.
3. To establish the authenticity the responsibility associated with the marketing functionaries in performing the marketing activities.
4. To evaluate the quality of performance in comparision with the preceding year.
5. To report to the management objectively the findings of the audit and to offer suitable suggestions towards better performance.

Approach and Scope of Marketing Audit

The approach towards marketing audit is to ensure commonality of the marketing functions in tune with the marketing goals. Usually the scope of marketing audit is determined by the management. The scope of marketing audit may be as below.

Macro Environment Audit

The audit is concerned with auditing macro environment consisting of demographic socio economic conditions determining the market conditions. This sort of audit provides deep insight into the market trend for the product

Micro Environment Audit

It deals with the characteristics of the target segment under consideration, the profile of the prospective buyers, competitors, dealers, transport and other facilitators operating in the micro level is audited.

Marketing Strategic Audit

Marketing strategic audit take into account of the objectives, policies in relation to the strategy adopted to market a product. Strategy audit include :

* Product strategy audit
* Promotion strategy audit
* Distribution strategy audit and
* Price strategy audit

Product Strategy Audit

This audit bring within its scope whether the company is making use of full resources available to the maximum extent possible etc.

Promotion Strategy Audit

Promotion strategy audit is concerned with media availability, media utilization, media effectiveness, elements of promotion mix, cost benefit analysis of the media employed and so on.

Distribution Strategy Audit

It deals with the mode of channel of distribution selected, benefit received and the channel efficiency.

Price Strategy Audit

It is concerned with pricing procedure adopted, suitability of such pricing strategy, evaluation of alternative price policies, pricing suitability in terms of product life cycle, pricing for new product and the related aspects.

Marketing Functional Audit

The scope of marketing functional audit is to know the effectiveness of marketing functions performed in relation to the marketing goals.

Marketing Efficiency Audit

The scope of marketing efficiency audit is to measure and determine the cost effectiveness associated with the performance of marketing functions.

Marketing Sales Force Audit

The scope of sales force audit is concerned with the procedure of estimating, selecting, appointing sales persons, their functions in relation to the objectives of sales promotion measures and the like.

Marketing Audit Programme

Marketing audit programme is a detailed plan of action indicating the work to be accomplished. The audit test and procedure to be adopted, duration of time required and such other details.

Marketing Audit Procedure

Marketing audit procedure involves the following sequence of operations.

1. Vouching

Vouching stands for verification of marketing activities performed in relation to the authority and authenticity of the functionaries who have performed such activities.

2. Confirmation

Confirmation is concerned with enduring the performance of marketing activity in relation to the short term and long term marketing objectives. Also it involves seeking supportive documentary evidence for the activities performed.

3. Reconciliation

It is concerned with seeking clarification from the marketing functionaries concerned under conditions where the activities are not in conformity with the results derived.

4. Scanning

Scanning is concerned with careful analysis of items which are to be reasonably probed further as to their accuracy and related aspects.

5. Reporting

It involves reporting to the top management the result of the audit programme carried out. Report usually includes measures suggested to improve the performance.

*** Requisite Qualification of a Marketing Auditor**

In addition to the basic qualities like honesty, fairness, tactfulness, diligence reliability and the like, a marketing auditor is normally required to possess the following other qualities to perform the job of auditing effectively.

* Product knowledge
* Knowledge of competitors
* Knowledge of government policies in relation to the business.

* Knowledge on advertisement and other promotion method.
* Knowledge of transport and communication
* Knowledge about consumers.

Merits of Marketing Audit

An organization can get the following merits by administrating marketing audit.

* Enables to understand the marketing efficiency in relation to each marketing activity.
* Marketing audit report provides guidelines for proceeding with future activity.
* Marketing audit facilitate reliability of the marketing data which form the basis for the future decision making.
* It act as a control technique that insist effective performance on the part of the marketing functionaries.

Limitations of Marketing Audit

The following limitations restrict the wider applicability of marketing audit.

1. Effectiveness of marketing operation can be generally known by means of other type of financial audit itself.
2. In view of combined nature of activities segregation of expenses pertaining to particular event or particular time is difficult.
3. Marketing strategies are influenced by environmental factors which are often subjected to change. Finding out of the duration of audit period itself is difficult.
4. Lack of professional audit personnel and procedure.
5. Suit to organization whose approach is marketing oriented.

Inspite of the limitations marketing audit has attracted the attention of marketing policy makers and the concept is accepted and practiced.

Marketing Information System

In order that the marketing activities are controlled effectively and meaningfully appropriate marketing information system is a must, as the information forms the basis for the action as well as corrective measures. In this context, a discussion on the marketing information system is presented below.

A systematic flow of information is a must for any managerial decisions. So also in marketing decisions. The accuracy of marketing decisions depends upon the reliable, understandable and timely information available. The purpose of marketing information system is to gather, process, analyze and disseminate information that will be of much greater value to the marketing personnel to arrive at appropriate marketing decisions.

Marketing information system has been defined by Samual Smit as "a continuing and interacting structure of people, equipment and procedure together, to analyze evaluate and distribute pertinent timely and accurate information for use by marketing decision makers to improve their planning, implementation and control." The American Marketing Association defines Marketing Information System as "a structured, interacting, complex of persons, machines and procedure designed to generate an orderly flow of pertinent information collected from intrafirm's and extrafirm's source for use as a basis for decision making in specific responsibility areas of marketing management."

Marketing information system is a part of overall management information system. Management information system is "a system of obtaining, storing, retrieving and anlysing data to produce information for use in planning, controlling, and decision making by yielding information for managers at the time they can most effectively use it".

Generally the marketing information system provides three types of information

(a) Environmental information which relate to the macro aspects linking government policies, political situation, climatic conditions etc.
(b) Competitive information which provide information pertaining to competitors behaviour in the market in terms of products, Price, Promotion and Distribution strategies and on related aspects.
(c) Internal information that represents information concerned with the internal functioning, strength, weakness, opportunities and threat within the firm.

The marketing personnel are in need of pertinent flow of information for the process of planning, control and for adhoc adjustments. Marketing information system is the base for any activity associated with marketing. The goal of marketing information system in a nutshell is to provide each marketing decision unit with information required to make accurate and appropriate decision, pertaining to his area of operation.

The Marketing Information required for personnel is different in view of the position of such personnel in the marketing department. Generally three main levels of personnel are identified.

Top level - where long range planning pertaining to marketing information is arrived

Middle level - where broad strategic plans are formulated by functional that are to move upon as per the marketing goal laid down by top level personnel and

Operation level - operation level which is responsible to carry out the plans laid down by the second level. Obviously the information requirement of each level is different.

Massy has identified three types of marketing information system.

(a) A library type : with the capacity to supply data on any question that may be presented.

(b) A system that feeds information into a well-specified models that are used to evaluate results, at different possible values of the independent variables and

(c) A system that produces data for models that help the personnel explore feasible solution to the problem.

All these three types of marketing information could exists at a time in an organization. The first and second type of marketing information will be most useful to the operation level personnel where as all those three types will be much useful to the top level personnel.

Development of Marketing Information Model

The Marketing Information System is developed in the following stages.

(1) Input data : The type of data required how, such data can be obtained are determined.

(2) Information Stores and Retrieval

The data so obtained are stored as to easily accessible for utilization.

(3) Analysis : The analysis being performed by following the procedural steps

* Definition of problem
* Determination of objectives
* Development of possible solutions
* Selection of optimum solution
* Implementation procedure

(4) Output : Analysis of information provides output in the form of reports, displays, graphs, charts, table etc.

(5) Decision making :

The output interpretation is given by the marketing personnel to arrive at meaningful inferences from the output and arrive decisions accordingly.

(6) Action : The decision taken for implementation is referred as the action and it is the solution arrived for the selected problem.

A simplified model of marketing information system is as shown in Exh. XI.

Flow Table

Application of Computer in Marketing Information System

The computers have emerged as a powerful aid to render and assist the marketing information system.

The application of computer in selected marketing areas is presented below :

1. Customer file processing on a sample basis

For the purpose of this programme several types of customers have been identified and customer numbers will be assigned. The programme CUST 1 is run in order to create a master file to which records may be added. This programme is also run to correct previous entries, delete old customers and to inquire individual record contents. The programme CUSTRPT1 is also used to provide means for printing reports form the file.

Exhibit X: Pyramid Effect of Responsibility

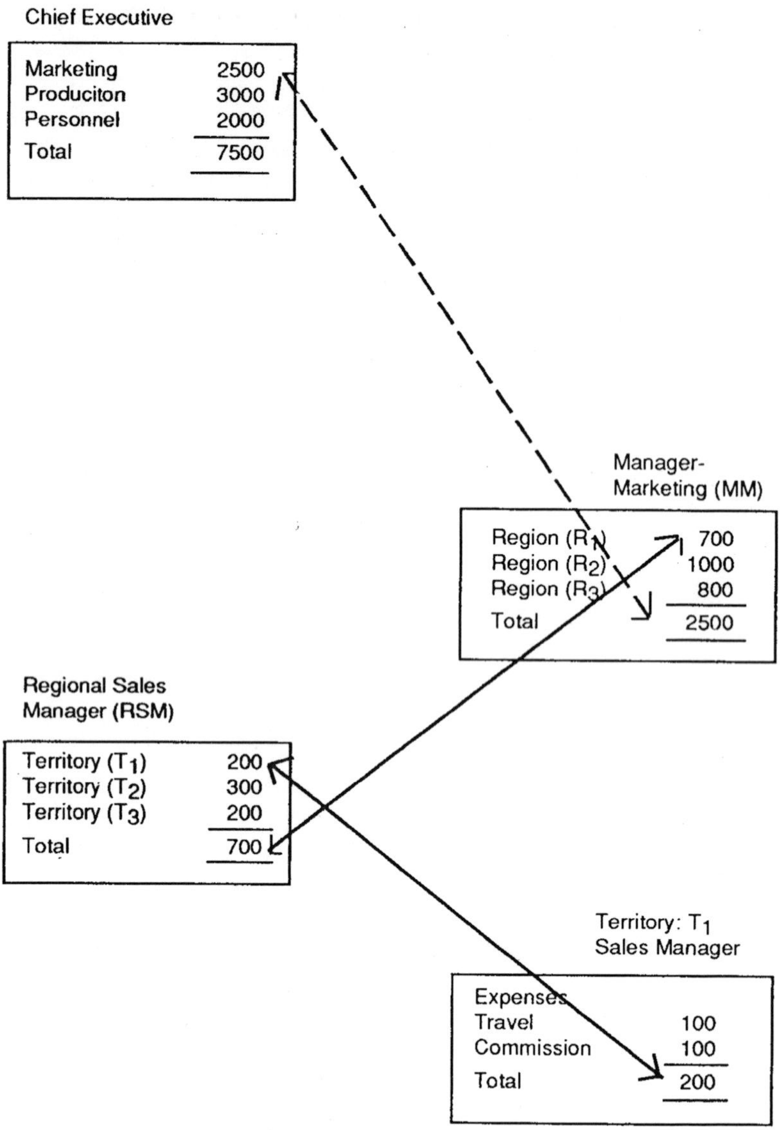

2. Advertising Response Analysis

The effectiveness or responses of the advertising campaign can be analyzed through the following programmes.

Adprol : which creates, adds and corrects information recorded for each response

Adpart : which produces reports on advertisement effectiveness.

3. Sales Commission Computation

For the purpose of sales commission computation the following files are being used.

Comm Data : which creates and maintain file of employee, sales transaction for each commission period.

Sman Prol : Maintains a file of information specific to each salesman

Comm Comp : which calculates commissions and produces reports following the end of each commission period.

The flow chart for computation of commission is shown below :

Salesmen Scheduling System The following programme enable salesman scheduling system Smansk 1 : Creates updates and print information in the master file. Smansk 2 : Updates the master file with the dates of orders received and date of new sales calls. Smansk 3 : Which prints reports from the master file in specified orders and formats The flow chart for salesman scheduling system is as shown in Ex. X.

6

Accounting for Marketing Personnel

Marketing personnel should be exposed to various accounting techniques and concepts. Such exposure will enable him to understand the financial implication of the decisions pertaining to their functional area. Among other things the marketing decisions are bound by financial considerations also. Obviously familiarity with regard to the concepts of accounting as well as an over all knowledge on the practical aspect are much imperative to the marketing personnel. On these account this topic presents an overview of the accounting aspects that will enable marketing personnel to gain insight into the practical aspects of accounting.

Accounting : The Conceptual Framework

Accounting according to American Institute of certified accountants "is the art of recording, classifying and summarizing in a significant manner in terms of monetary transactions the events which are in part at least of financial character and interpreting the results thereof. This definition shows that accounting is concerned with recording of events which are financial nature to present a picture to the people concerned as regards the financial status of the organisation. The people concerned with accounting statements are shareholders, creditors and the general public.

The accounting records are based on concepts, conventions and principles laid down by specialised bodies involve in accounting profession. The major concepts of accounting are :

1. Business Entity Concept

This refers to a clear distinction between business and the owner's of the business. Business transaction are to be viewed from the business point of view and not from the owners of the business point of view.

2. Money Measurement Concept

As per this concept only those events that can be expressed in quantitative terms are to be recorded. Also it means all those events that are to be converted into monetary terms are recorded and not otherwise in any other form.

3. Cost Concept

The transactions are recorded in terms of its original cost and not in terms of the worth of it.

4. Going Concern Concept

This concept refers to the continuous operation of business without being closed down. On this basis the accounting transactions are recorded on a long term indefinite perspective.

5. Dual Aspect Concept

As per this concept each event has two aspects viz., the receiving aspect as well as the giving aspect. Acquisition of an asset is a receiving aspect which is concerned with the giving aspect of parting with the money value of the asset or parting with another asset.

6. Realisation Concept

Accounting is a record of past events. It is not prepared on anticipatory basis but prepared on the basis of occurrence of the events.

7. Accrual Basis

Usually in accounting one business transaction has taken place means its consequence is likely to continue for a future period. The profit/loss will arise only out of the consequential operation and such operations will result into increase or decrease in the owners equity.

In addition to the concept above the conventions usually practiced are :

Consistency i.e., uniformity in relation to maintenance of accounting records.

Disclosure i.e., disclosure of all significant information other than what to be exposed legally.

Conservatism i.e., concerned with presenting the financial position as it is without assinging a better or worse position than the actual so that accounting records will show a true state of affairs of the business.

The accounts are classified under three heads, personal, real and nominal accounts. Personal accounts are concerned with individual, company's etc., Real accounts are concerned with items such as assets and Nominal accounts are concerned with expenses and income. The basic accounting rules applicable to the three types accounts are :

Personal Account	:	Debit the receiver and credit the giver
Real Account	:	Debit what comes in and credit what goes out
Nominal account	:	Debit all expenses and losses credit all incomes and gains

In the matter of a person, "debit : refers to that he has received some benefits against which he has rendered some service or will render the service in future. In the matter of goods, debit refers to the fact that the value of such goods has increased and the matter of other accounts the firm has enjoyed some benefits or has lost money.

A "credit" in case of person refers to some benefits has been received from him, entitling him to claim from the firm a return benefit in the form of cash or service. In the case of goods or properties that the value has diminished and in case of other accounts the firm had made some gain.

Financial Accounting Records

Financial accounting records are those that are concerned with the historical records of the business events on monetary basis. The financial records shows the result of the business operations for a specific accounting period usually twelve months.

A brief description of the important financial accounting records are as below :

1. Journal

Journal is a book of original entry wherein the transactions are recorded as and when they occur. The process of recording is known as journalising. Journal involves classification of the accounts, application of accounting rules and then debiting/ crediting as the case it may be. The form of a journal is as below :

Journal

Date	Particulars	L.F.	Debit Rs.	Credit Rs.

2. Ledger

Ledger accounts are being prepared on the basis of entries in the journal. In the journal the transaction are recorded as and when they occur. In the ledger such transactions are recorded under convenient heads of accounts so as to group them and extract balances easily.

A proforma of two ledger accounts are presented below :

Personal Accounts

Dr							Cr
Date	Particulars	J.F.	Amount	Date	Particulars	J.F.	Amount

Rent Account

Dr							Cr
Date	Particulars	J.F.	Amount	Date	Particulars	J.F.	Amount

3. Trial Balance

Trial balance is a statement of balances showing debits and credits separately. The total of the debit column and credit column should agree. An agreement indicates the mathematical accuracy of the accounts prepared. The agreement arise from the fact that, under double entry system of accounting the debit side of the accounts will always be equal to the credit side.

All illustrated example of Journal, ledger and trial balance are as follows :

1.	Commenced business with capital	10,000
2.	Purchased goods	5,000
3.	Sold goods to Arun & Co.	2,000
4.	Sold goods for cash	1,000
5.	Goods returned by Arun & Co.	500

Journal Entries

Date	Particulars		Rs.	Rs.
1.	Cash A/c	Dr	10,000	
	To capital A/c			10,000
	(Being capital introducted in business)			
2.	Purchase A/c	Dr	5,000	
	To cash A/c			5,000
	(Being goods purchased for cash)			
3.	Arun & Co. A/c	Dr	2,000	
	To Sales A/c			2,000
	(Being goods sold to M/s. Arun & Co.)			
4.	Cash A/c	Dr	1,000	
	To Sales A/c	Dr		1,000
	(Being goods sold for cash)			
5.	Sales Return A/c	Dr	500	
	To Arun & Co. A/c			500
	(Being the goods sold returned)			

Ledger A/cs

Capital A/c

Date	Particulars	JF	Amount	Date	Particluars	JF	Amount
31.12	To balance c/d		10,000		By cash		10,000
					By balance b/d		10,000

Cash A/c

Date	Particulars	JF	Amount	Date	Particulars	JF	Amount
1	To capital		10,000	2	By Purchases		5,000
4	To sales		1,000	31.	By balance c/d		6,000
			11,000				11,000
	To balance b/d		6000				

Arun & Co. A/c

Date	Particulars	JF	Amount	Date	Particulars	JF	Amount
	To sales		2,000		By Sales returns		500
					By bal c/d		1,500
			2,000				2,000
	To balance b/d		1,500				

Sales Return A/c

Date	Particulars	JF	Amount	Date	Particulars	JF	Amount
	To Arun & Co. A/c		500		By balance c/d		500
			500				500
	To bal b/d		500				

Sales A/c

Date	Particulars	JF	Amount	Date	Particulars	JF	Amount
	To bal c/d		3,000		By Arun & Co. A/c		2,000
					By cash A/c		1,000
			3,000				3,000
					By balance b/d		3,000

Trial Balance

Particulars	Debit	Credit
Capital A/c		10,000
Purchases A/c	5,000	
Sales A/c		3,000
Sales returns A/c	500	
Cash A/c	6,000	
Arun & Co. A/c	1,5000	
	13, 000	13,000

Subsidary Financial Accounting Record

The following are the major subsidiary financial accounting records

Purchase Book

The purchase book contains the record of credit purchases. The proforma of purchase book is presented below :

Date	Particulars	L.F.	Details	Amount

The particular column is meant to record the name of the supplier, the name of the article purchased and the respective quantities. The amount in respect of each article is entered in the details column after totalling of the various amounts included in single purchase, the net amount is included in the total column.

Sales Book

The sales book is a register specially kept to record the credit sales of goods dealt by the firm. The proforma of sales book is given below

Date	Particulars	L.F.	Details	Amount

In the particulars column name of the customer and the details relating to quantities of goods sold will be recorded. For each item the amount is entered in the detail column. The total of the particular column will show the credit sales for the period.

Purchase Returns Book

This book records the return of goods purchased to the suppliers. However if the returns are insignificant it may be sufficient to record transactions in the Journal itself. The proforma of purchase return is similar to that of the purchase book.

Sales Returns Book

If customers frequently return the goods sold to them it will be convenient to record the return in a separate book called as sales returns book. The forms of the book is the same as the sales book.

Cash Book

In the cash book the cash transactions are straight away recorded and cash book itself servers as the cash account ledger bank account ledger. It is the part of a ledger account also. The cash book may be of three types.

* Simple cash book : With one amount column on the receipt as well as on the payment side.
* Double column cash book : In this book along with the amount column on the receipt and payment side discount allowed as well as discount received will also be entered.
* Three Column cash book : In the three column cash book both in the receipt side and in the payment side the amount in bank and in hand, also the discount received and paid will appear.

Proforma of the three types of cash books are presented below :

Simple Cash Book

Date	Receipts	LF	Amount	Date	Payments	LF	Amount

Double Cash Book

Date	Receipts	LF	Discount	Cash	Date	Particulars	LF	Discount	Cash

Three Column Cash Book

Date	Receipts	LF	Discount	Cash	Bank	Date	Particulars	LF	Discount	Cash	Bank

Trading and Profit and Loss Account and Balance Sheet

At the end of each financial year trading and profit and loss account and balance sheet is prepared. The trading account aims to find out the gross profit. The trading account incorporate the opening stock, purchases and purchase related expenses, sales and closing stock. The profit and loss account aims to find out the net profit which incorporates all expenses and the income.

The balance sheet is a statement showing assets and liabilities which is prepared to portray the financial position. The assets are presented in the form of fixed assets and current assets. The liabilities in the form of owners equity, long term liability, short term liability.

Cost Accounting

Cost accounting as defined by the institute of cost and management accounts England as "the application of costing and cost accounting principles, methods and techniques to the presentation of information derived there from for the purpose of managerial decision making".

Cost accounting is thus a record for cost. It begins with the recording of income and expenditure and with presentation of statistical data. Cost accounting enable cost determination and measurement and also it helps for cost planning and control.

From the marketing personnels point of view cost accounting is particularly helpful in the following aspects :

* To determine cost per unit and cost structure of each product or services carried out by the firm.
* To enable product pricing.
* To identify and prevent areas of wastage in utilisation of resources.
* To provide cost information for market decisions.
* To ascertain profitability of each product.

* To provide cost data for submission of tenders or contracts.
* To advise on product expansion or deletion decision making.
* To make decisions on
    * make/buy from outside
    * Shutdown or continue to operation
    * replacement
* To formulate marketing strategy.

Cost Component

From the cost accounting point of view functionally the total cost of a product consists of prime cost, works cost, cost of sales and selling price. The cost analysis is presented below :

Classification	Component
Prime cost	Direct material
	Direct labour
	Direct expenses
Factory Cost	Prime cost
	Indirect factory expense
	Factory cost
Cost of Production	Factory cost
	Indirect administration expense
Cost of Sales	Cost of production
	Selling expenses

Cost Sheet

The analysis of different element of cost is shown in the statement and such statement is known as cost sheet. Cost sheet is a schedule or document which provides for presentation of the estimated detailed cost in respect of cost centre or cost unit. A proforma of cost sheet is given below :

Cost Sheet for the Period
Direct Material

* Opening stock
* Purchases
* Carriage inwards

* Direct material
* Direct wages
* Direct expenses

Prime Cost

Add : Indirect material
Indirect wages
Rent and rates
Lighting and heating
Power and fuel
Repairs and maintenance
Cleaning
Other expense
Cost of research
Depreciation
Work stationary
State insurance
Welfare service
Insurance
Loose tools
Works manager's salary

Works of Factory Cost

Add : Office administrative overhead
Rent and rate
Salaries
Lighting and heating
Insurance
Cleaning
Telephone
Printing
Depreciation
Legal expenses
Audit fee
Bank charges

Cost of Production

Add : Selling and distribution
Show room rent
Lighting and heating
Salesmen salary

Commission
Travel expenses
Printing
Advertising
Bad debts
Directors fee
Postage
Depreciation
Debt collection expenses
Carriage
Freight outward
Samples

Cost of Sales

Add : Net profit or
Less : Net loss
Sales

Accounting for Materials

Accounting for materials under cost accounting assumes importance, as the material cost occupies significant portion of the total cost. The material that is to be maintained at any time is generally fixed taking into account of the following levels :

1. Maximum level
2. Minimum level
3. Order level
4. Re-order level
5. Danger level
6. Economic ordering quantity

Maximum Level

The maximum level is the level of material which can be held in stock at any time. The maximum level takes into account of average rate of consumption, availability of money, storage space, the lead time and the economic ordering quantity.

Maximum level = Reorder level + reorder quantity – (Minimum consumption × minimum reorder period)

Minimum Level

The minimum level represents the quantity below which the inventory of any item should not be allowed to fall. The minimum stock levels fixed by considering reorder level, lead time, average rate of consumption and the like.

The formula used to determine the minimum levels

Minimum level = Reorder level – (Normal consumption × Normal reorder period)

Reorder Level

Reorder level is the reordering of stock level in relative to an item of stock. It is the point at which it is essential to initiate purchase orders. Reorder level is fixed by considering average rate of consumption, lead time and economic ordering quantity. The formula for reorder level is

Reorder level = Maximum period x maximum usage period or week.

Danger Level

Danger level represents a stage where immediate steps are to be taken for getting the stock replenished. When the stock reaches the danger level it indicate that if no emergency steps are taken to restock the materials the stores will be completely exhausted and the normal function will be stopped.

Economic Ordering Quantity

Economic ordering quantity is that quantify its optimum for placing order from a supplier. Such optimum approach has to be followed by balancing the ordering cost against the holding cost. The equation for calculation of economic ordering quantity's.

EOQ = 2AS/I

where

EOQ = Economic reordering quantity

A = Annual usage in units

S = Ordering cost for one order

I = Inventory carrying cost per unit

ABC Analysis

The material will be classified into three categories for the purpose of exercising selective control on materials. An analysis of the material costs will show that a smaller percentage of items of material cost will contribute to a larger percentage of the value of consumption and on the other hand to larger percentage of items may represent a smaller percentage of value of items consumed. Between these two extremes will fall those items the percentage of which is more or less equal to their value of consumption. Items falling in the first category are treated as "A" items, of the second category "B" items and the third category are "C" items. Such an analysis is known as ABC analysis. This is otherwise known as Always Better Control Analysis or Proportional Parts Value analysis.

VED Analysis

VED stands for Vital, Essential and Desirable. This is used primarily for control of spare parts which are divided into three categories as above. The spares the stockout of which even for a short time will stop production is known as vital and those spares the absence cannot be tolerated for more than few hours or a day is grouped as essential and the desirable spares are those spares which are needed but their absence even for a week or so will not lead to stoppage of production. The VED analysis is being performed to get the stock control very effective.

Valuation of Materials

The material valuation is concerned with fixation of the material issue prices from the stores for production. There are many methods of pricing material issues. The prominent methods are :

Cost Price Methods

Fist in first out
Last in first out
Average cost
Inflated price
Specific price
Base stock
Highest in first out

Market Price Methods

Replacement price
Realizable value

Standard Price Methods

Current standard price
Basic standard price

Under first in first out method the material is first issued from the earliest consignment on hand and priced at the cost at which that consignment was placed in the stores. Whereas in the case of last in first out method the issues are priced in the reverse order of purchase i.e., the prices of the latest available consignment is taken.

As regards the average cost methods concerned all the materials in store is mixed up that an issue cannot be made from any particular lot of purchases i.e., the prices of the latest available consignment is taken.

As regards the average cost method is concerned all the materials in share is mixed up that an issue cannot be made from any particular lot of purchases and therefore the price of the material is fixed on average basis. The average may be simple average or weighted arithmetic average. A simple average means the price is calculated by dividing the total prices of the material in stock from which the material to pieces used in that total.

Weighted arithmetic average means "a price which is calculated by dividing the total cost of material in the stock from which the material to be priced could be drawn by the total quantity of materials in that stock".

The weighted average price take into account the price as well as the quantity of materials in store.

The inflated price method is used where the product is subject to wastage on loading and unloading. Inflated price refers to price higher than the actual price, so as to recover the natural wastage of material where the materials are purchased for specific job or for specific work order. They should be issued to the specific job at their actual cost. Under that circumstances the specific price is used.

Base stock method is used in the concerns which maintains a minimum of material in stock. The minimum is known as safety or base stock means for using only under emergency. The base stock is created out of the first lot of the material purchased and therefore it is always valued at the cost price of the first lot and is carried forward as a fixed asset.

Highest in First out Method

The highest in first out method is based on the assumption that the closing stock of material showed always remain at the minimum value. So the issues are priced as the highest value of the available consignment in the store.

Market price methods may be either replacement price or realisation price. The replacement price is used in case of items which are held in stock for use in production while realisable price is used in respect of the items which are kept in stock for sale. Generally market price methods considered to be the best method where quotation have to be sent that would reflect the latest competitive conditions.

As regards the standard price method are concerned it is a predetermined price and both the receipts and issues will be valued as this price. The difference between actual price and standard price is charged to an account known as purchase price variance account.

Marketing Research and Development Accounting

The accounting for research and development is gaining ground in view of the significance associated with research and development. The major objective behind this accounting is

1. To maintain company's present competitive position and profits by keeping the existing products competitive in terms of quality and price.

2. Improving company's present competitive position by developing new products and improving existing products.

3. To explore the possibilities of new field of funds to be utilised for substantial profit.

The accounting treatment pertaining to research and development is of two types.

1. Capitalization Method

Under this method the research and development cost are allocated over a period of ten years in which anticipated benefits therefrom are expectful to be reaped. Research and development cost are treated as deferred revenue expenditure which is to be charged to the income statement for a number of years. This method is also known as deferred method and recommended where in the investment in research and development is more and where benefit expected is to follow for a number of years.

2. Revenue Method

Under this method the general research and related cost incurred for betterment of exiting products improvement process, plant layout etc to be charged to the cost of goods sold by directly allocating them to specific products or job or else treated as overheads to be recovered through general overhead absorption rates.

The institute of cost and works accounts Calcutta suggested the following objectives to be incorporated in research and development cost.

1. Improvement of existing cost
2. Improvement of existing method of production
3. Searching for new product
4. Searching for new method of production
5. New application of material

The following cost activities are to be included in research and development cost as per the International Accounting Standards Committee.

1. Salaries and wages and other related expenses of research personnel.
2. The cost of material and services on research activities.
3. Depreciation of research equipments.
4. Amortization cost of patterns licenses etc pertaining to research.

Tools for Financial Analysis and Control

Marketing personnel has to be exposed to tools meant for financial analysis and control. By being exposed to such tools the

the decision will be more appropriate. Important financial tools are :

1. Fund flow analysis
2. Cash flow analysis
3. Ratio analysis
4. Break even analysis
5. Financial analysis through leverages

Fund Flow Analysis

Fund constitutes the prime importance in starting and operating any business. Marketing decisions are concerned with the flow of funds from various sources and application of funds. Fund is defined in the sense of spending power. It refers to the value embedded in assets. Funds are usually received into a business, initially in the term of cash and cash related items. Funds do not seize to exist merely because cash has been transformed into assets. The fund statement answer to questions such as where profit has gone, what is the increase or decrease in the current assets position? How a debt has been retired ? What is the position of opening stock and so on. Thus a fund flow statement is an important statement reflecting on the financial position.

Fund flow statement is also described as a statement of sources and application of funds. The purpose of this statement is to show as to how funds flow between different assets and equity items during an accounting period. Preparation of fund flow statement involves the following steps.

1. Preparation of statement showing changes in working capital.
2. Preparation of statement to calculate depreciation on fixed assets.
3. Ascertain funds from operation by adding in deducting the following items from Net profit.

Items to be Added to Net Profits

1. Depreciation
2. Deferred revenue expenditure
3. Loss on sale of fixed assets

Items to be Deducted from Net Profits

1. Gain on sale of fixed assets
2. Income tax payment

4. Identification of sources and uses.

Sources

* Fund from operation
* Decrease in fixed assets
* Increase in liabilities
* Proceeds from the sale of securities
* Sale of investments
* Non trading items (dividend received)

Application

* Loss from operation
* Increase in fixed asset
* Decrease in liabilities
* Redemption of securities
* Purchase of fixed assets
* Cash dividends
* Non trading expenses (Interest on borrowings)
* Increase in working capital

5. Comparing the sources with application one will arrive at the flow of fund.

Cash Flow Analysis

Cash flow is the receipt as well as the payments of cash that implies the movement of cash. It also reflects to the sum of net income and those of non fund charges, all the type of amortrized and book transfers which do not affect the total quantity of funds in use. Cash flow embodies a detailed picture of sources of cash receipt and uses. Cash flow statement excludes transactions which do not involve cash. Also cash flow statement ignore accrued concepts, only the receiving and payment effect is considered, cash flow statement enable for remedial measures with reference to supplies or shortage of cash.

Financial Analysis Through Leverages

Leverage is an advantage or disadvantage which is derived from earning a return on total investment and which is different from return on owners equity. The following are the types of leverages.

1. Return on investment leverage
2. Assets leverage
3. Operating leverage
4. Financial leverage
5. Total leverage
6. Fixed charges leverage
7. Combined leverage

1. Return on Investment Leverage

Return on investment is an important indicator of the firms performance of operational efficiency return on investment leverage is found by means of

$$\frac{\text{Sales}}{\text{Total asset}} \times \text{Profit margin}$$

2. Asset Leverage

Assets turnover indicates the performance of business. A firm with relatively high turnover is said to have high degree of asset leverage. Asset leverage enable inter firm performance.

3. Operating Leverage

Operating leverage takes place when change in the revenue produces greater changes in earnings before int

and tax (EBIT). The operating leverage will usually be the highest near the break even point.

$$\text{Operating leverage} = \frac{\text{Marginal contribution}}{\text{EBIT}}$$

$$= \frac{\text{Marginal contribution}}{\text{Revenue–Variable cost–Fixed cost}}$$

4. Financial Leverage

Financial leverage depends upon the ratio of debt and preferred stock equity. There are three ratio's which determined the degree of financial ratio.

$$\text{Debt equity ratio} = \frac{\text{Debt}}{\text{Equity}}$$

$$\text{Debt ratio} = \frac{\text{Total debt}}{\text{Total assets}}$$

$$\text{Time interest concerned ratio} = \frac{\text{EBIT}}{\text{Annual interest charges}}$$

The extent of financial leverage may be measured by the following ratio.

$$= \frac{\text{Percentage changes in earnings after tax}}{\text{Percentage changes in EBIT}}$$

5. Total Leverage

The total extent of a firms leverage may be measured with the following formula

Degree of total leverage = Degree of operating leverage × Degree of financial leverage

6. Fixed Charges Leverage

The fixed cost leverage indicates the extent to which changes in operating income affect the earnings before interest and taxes. It is calculated by formula :

$$\frac{\text{EBIT}}{\text{EBT}}$$

or

$$\frac{\text{Revenue-Variable cost-Fixed cost}}{\text{Revenue–Variable cost–Fixed cost–Interest}}$$

7. Combined Leverage

Combined leverage compares revenues with changes in EBT.

The formula for combined leverages is

Combined leverage = Operating leverage × Fixed charge leverage

$$= \frac{\text{Marginal contribution}}{\text{EBIT}} \times \frac{\text{EBIT}}{\text{EBT}}$$

$$= \frac{\text{Revenue–Variable cost}}{\text{Revenue–VC–FC–Interest charges}}$$

Value Analysis

Value analysis is the organized and exhaustively critical study of a product in terms of design functions, and costs with the objects of cost reduction.

Value analysis is quite familiar now-a-days as this enable savings of cost in the performance of marketing activities without any sacrifice of the efficiency associated therewith in the performance. It is essentially a programme for wringing costs from a product by analysing the material, design and manufacturing process, employed in the production. Value analysis is a systematic comparison and analytical approach which enable a firm to get value for the money spent. Many times value engineering is associated with value analysis. The difference between the two rest upon the point that while value engineering is considered as cost avoidance and value analysis is concerned with cost reduction.

In the marketing context value analysis has definite application in the areas such as product planning and development, purchasing operations, distribution strategy and the like.

With regard to value analyses pertaining to product planning and designing the manufacturer has to identify the three value—"use value" "esteem value" and "cost value". The use value is determined by the features of the product which render the expected specific benefit to the users. The esteem value is associated with the additional benefits the products can offer to the user and the cost value is concerned with the cost of manufacturing of the product that include material cost, labour cost, overheads and other direct and indirect costs. The above three values may be equated with price. Accordingly the exchange value is the price the buyer offer to the total values of use, esteem and cost. The difference between the cost value and the exchange value will result into profit or loss as the case it may be.

With respect to product addition of deletion the manufacturer should think in terms of functional value as well as utilisation value. The functional value refers to evaluation of specifications, qualifications or design of a product against the background of what is required to be achieved through the available particular resource. The utilisation value on the other hand determines the extend to which an effective use is made of the specified resources.

The process of value analysis, incorporates the following sequences :

1. Selection of product to be analysed
2. Obtaining the cost of the product
3. Recording the number of components
4. Recording all the functions
5. Recording the number of components currently and the forcible future
6. Determination of primary functions
7. Assigning the cost of all the alternatives
8. Evaluating the cheapest alternatives
9. Decision of further inclusions in the product

The actual explorations in cost reduction are based on the familiar method of questioning. Following are the questions pertaining to product :

1. Can any part in the product be eliminated ?
2. Can the parts be separated ?
3. Can standards parts be used ?
4. Can cheap material be used ?
5. Can less material be used ?
6. Can the present material be purchased cheaply ?
7. Can the reflections be reduced ?
8. Can limitations be adopted ?
9. Can the alternative materials be used ?
10. Can the alternative methods be used ?
11. Can risk be minimised ?
12. Can the resources be put to better use ?

The objects of value analysis are as below :

1. To simplify products

2. To use cheaper but better materials
3. To introduce efficient process
4. To reduce cost of production
5. To improve the product design
6. To increase utility of product
7. To increase profit

Value analysis is thus an effective technique towards cost reduction. This analysis assumes significance in the growing competitive market conditions where the competitors are competing with almost similar brand features. Under that situation any reduction in the price will induce the buyer to prefer such brand. Price reduction obviously involve cost control which in turn can be effectively handled by means of value analysis. Thus value analysis is a valuable tool towards effective marketing operation.

Ratio Analysis

Ratio analysis serves as important tool of financial analysis, as ratio makes the related information comparable. The ratios are usually classified under four heads namely.

1. Liquidity ratios
2. Capital structure ratios
3. Profitability ratio and
4. Activity ratio

Ratio's are used as a device to analyse and interpret the financial soundness of the organisation concerned. For the marketing personnel ratio analysis is important in view of the following benefits :

* It gives the financial trend in a simplified form
* It enables a comparative analysis
* It facilitates intra firm comparison
* It enables predicting the future behavior
* It enables control.

Liquidity Ratio

The liquidity ratio's usually measure the ability of the firm to meet its short term obligation and reflect the short term financial strength and Solvency. The important liquidity ratios are current ratio and quick or acid test ratio.

Current ratio refers to the relationship between current assets and current liabilities. It is a quantitative index of the liquidity position. The formula for current ratio is,

$$\text{Current ratio} = \frac{\text{Current asset}}{\text{Current liability}}$$

The quick ratio is the relation between quick asset and quick liability.

$$\text{Quick ratio} = \frac{\text{Quick asset}}{\text{Quick liability}}$$

Quick ratio is also called as acid test ratio as it is concerned as the acid to test the financial soundness.

Quick assets = Current assets – (Stock + Prepaid expenses)

Quick liability = Current liabilities – Bank overdraft

The capital structure ratio is concerned with the long term solvency of a firm as to its ability to assure the long term creditors in relation to periodic payment. There are two types of capital structure ratio.

Debt Equity Ratio : This ratio establishes the relationship between share holders fund and outsiders fund.

$$\text{Debt equity ratio} = \frac{\text{Debt}}{\text{Equity}} \text{ or } \frac{\text{Outside liability}}{\text{Inside liability}}$$

Proprietary Ratio

Proprietary ratio is the relationship between proprietors funds and total tangible assets.

$$\text{Proprietary ratio} = \frac{\text{Share holders funds}}{\text{Total tangible assets}}$$

Profitability ratio's on the other hand enable to measure the profit position of the firm. The profitability ratio may be based on sales which includes margin ratio's which are

$$\text{Gross profit ratio} = \frac{\text{Gross profit}}{\text{Sales}}$$

$$\text{Net profit ratio} = \frac{\text{Gross profit}}{\text{Sales}}$$

The profitability ratios related to investments include

$$\text{Return on asset ratio} = \frac{\text{Total assets}}{\text{Capital employed}}$$

$$\text{Return on capital employed} = \frac{\text{Net profit + interest + tax}}{\text{Capital employed}}$$

Return on shareholders equity including earnings per share, dividend per share, dividend pay out ratio, earnings and dividends yield.

Return on investment ratios is found by the following formulas

$$\frac{\text{Profit before taxes}}{\text{Sales}} \times \frac{\text{Sales}}{\text{Equity capital}}$$

Return on equity on the other hand is found as

$$\text{Return on total equity} = \frac{\text{Net profit after taxes}}{\text{Total stock holders equity}}$$

The activity ratios are known as efficiency ratios or turnover ratios. They are a test of relationship between sales and cost of goods sold. Activity ratio may be

$$\text{Stock turn over ratio} = \frac{\text{Cost of goods sold}}{\text{Average stock}}$$

$$\text{Debtors turnover ratio} = \frac{\text{Debotrs + BIR}}{\text{Credit sales}} \times \text{number of working days}$$

$$\text{Creditors turnover ratio} = \frac{\text{Sales}}{\text{Net fixed assets}}$$

In addition to the above ratios there are a number of miscellaneous ratios. The following chart summarizes the possible various key ratios to predict the financial and finance related efficiency of a firm based on net profit.

Capital Budgeting

Capital budgeting decisions are concerned with long term investment of the firm's concerned. Such decisions once taken cannot be revised so easily. As such the marketing operations to a greater extent are governed by capital budgeting decisions. Therefore knowledge about capital budgeting is much imperative to the marketing personnel. The specific reasons as to why the marketing personnel must be acquainted with capital budgeting are as below :

* The volume of production and the type of production, is influenced by capital budgeting.
* Product planning innovation and development and the related activities are determined to a great extent by capital budgeting.
* A firm is financially committing for a longer period. The capital budgeting is a decision making process by which firm evaluate the purchases of major fixed assets including building, machinery and equipments. The capital budgeting proposal incorporated the following

1. Replacement

Refers to the process of worn out and obsolete equipment being replaced.

2. Expansion

Refers to expanding activities in terms of production, sales, additional capacity, utilisation and so on so as to expand the volume of production.

3. Modernisation

These decisions are concerned with upgradation of capital, making it modernised equipments and thereby reducing cost.

4. Strategic Investment

Concerned with returns on a long term future basis. The aim of such strategic investment is to ensure the firm's future growth.

5. Diversification

It is related to operating in several markets with more than one product lines.

6. Research and Development

Keeping in pace with changing conditions the research and development activities will take place to reap the benefits on a future period of time.

Capital Budgeting Techniques

The techniques of capital budgeting are as below :

1. Pay Back Period

It is concerned with the length of the time required to recover the investment from the firm's cash flow.

$$\text{Pay back period} = \frac{\text{Investment}}{\text{Net annual cash flow}}$$

2. Average Rate of Return

Average rate of return enables to find the alternative uses of available fund. The firm has to select the most favorable product based on average rate of return.

$$= \frac{\text{Cash flow–depreciation–Interest}}{\text{Investment}} \times \frac{\text{Number of projects}}{\text{Number of years}}$$

3. Internal Rate of Return

It is the rate which equates the present value of the expected future cash flow with the cost of investment.

Internal rate of return

Formula

$$ {}_{t=1}^{n} \frac{Ct}{(+10)^{t}} $$

Where C_t is the cash flow of each profit after tax but before depreciation and interest period.

'r' is the rate of discount

4. Net Present Worth

It deals with the present value of the fund in hand than its future value which is subject to uncertainty and risk. The net present worth of the expected net cash flow of each project which is obtained by discounting the net cash flow of each project by a discount rate which equals the firm's cost of capital.

Formula

$$ {}_{t=1}^{n} \frac{C'_t}{(1+k)^{t}} - {}_{t=1}^{n} \frac{CO_t}{(1+k)^{t}} $$

C'_t = net cash flow in year
k = Firms cost of capital
CO_t = Cost of investment in year t
n = Proposal's life in years

5. Profitability Index

The profitability index exhibits the relationship between the present values of net cash inflows and the present values of cash outflows.

Formula

$$ P_1 = \frac{E^{n}_{t=1} \frac{CO_t}{(1+k)^{t}}}{{}_{t=1}^{n} \frac{CO_t}{(1+k)^{t}}} $$

P_1 = Profitability index

C't = net cash flow in year t
k = the firms cost of capital
CO_t = cost of investment in year t
n = the proposals life in years

6. Discounted Rate of Return Method

The formula for discounted rate of return is

$$\frac{F_1}{(1+r)^1} + \frac{F_2}{(1+r)^2} + \text{-------} + \frac{F^n}{(1+r)^n} + \frac{S}{(1+r)^n}$$

C = the supply price of asset
F = the future cash inflow
S = the salvage value
r = the discounted rate of return

The discounted cash flow method recognizes that the use of money has a cost also it signifies cash inflows and outflows rather than net income.

In addition to the above methods there are many more methods that are available to evaluate the capital budgeting proposal. The decision on capital budgeting is more challenging under conditions of risk and uncertainties. As such capital budgeting are influenced by many other considerations other than pure financial consideration.

Inflation Accounting

In view of the limitations of historical cost based accounting, marketers are to be exposed to the inflation accounting which are more relevant and showing fairly accurate financial position in tune with the present conditions. The historical cost based accounting records suffers from the problems which are mainly three.

1. Current revenue is not matched with the current cost of operation.
2. The cost of goods sold is usually understated.
3. The historical cost based depreciation is not enough to maintain the operating capability of the enterprise.

It is to be stated here that the inflation accounting is in its infant stage and no single method has gained universal acceptance. However these aspects draw specific attention in the context of inflation accounting.

1. Periodic revaluation of assets along with adoption of LIFO method of closing stock revaluation. This will considerably reduce the impact of changing prices. Such revaluation is to be performed on a regular interval of 2 to 4 years.
2. Current purchasing power accounting by that efforts are to be taken to eliminate the effect of changes in the value of money itself. The current purchasing power accounting basically attempts to remove the changes in the pricing due to inflation or deflation as the case may be.
3. Current cost accounting is another aspect of inflationary accounting. The main features of current cost accounting are:
   a. Money will continue to be the basic feature of measurement.
   b. Assets and liabilities will be shown in the business at their value to the business.
   c. Profit for the year is arrived at after changing the value to the business of assets concerned during the period which involves depreciation adjustment, cost of sales adjustment and monetary working capital adjustment.

Human Resource Accounting

The basic point with respect to human resource accounting is that it treats investment in human resources as assets. Human resource accounting may be defined as the measurement and reporting of the cost and value of people as organisational resources.

The major assumptions underlying human resource accounting include

1. that people are valuable organisational resources.
2. that the value of people is influenced by management style.

Human resource accounting has two major aspects

1. Human resource cost accounting.
2. Human resource value accounting.

Human resource cost accounting refers to the cost of personnel activities and functions such as recruitment selection, hiring, replacement and training. Human resource value accounting refers to accounting for the cost of people as human assets. Human resource cost may be defined as the sacrifice incurred to acquire or replace people.

Human resource cost also includes :

a. Historical Cost

The cost incurred to.acquire and develop people.

b. Replacement Cost

The cost to be incurred to replace the human resources presently employed.

The above two costs include recruitment cost, selection costs, development cost and so on.

The major objectives behind human resource accounting is to provide managers feedback information on their performance and to plan properly for manpower related activities.

Exhibit XI: Marketing Audit Programme

Function	*Product Planning*	*Pricing*	*Sales Persons*	*Market Research*	*Advertising*	*Distribution*	*Storage*	*Transport*	*Budgeting*
Jan.									
Feb.									
Mar.									
Apr.									
May.									
Jun.									
Jul.									
Aug.									
Sep.									
Oct.									
Nov.									
Dec.									

Exhibit XII: Ratios in Reaction to Net Profit

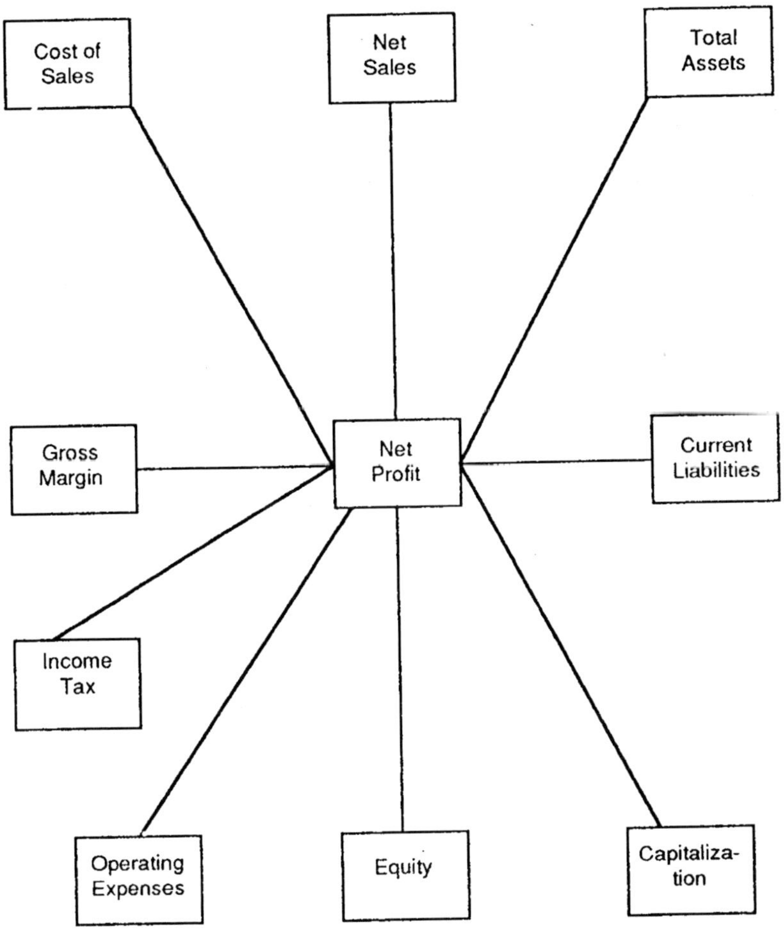

Bibliography

Arch. W. Troelstrup—Consumer problems and personal fiance.

Bhabatosh Banerjee—Cost Accounting.

David, A. Akker and James G Meyers—Advertising management

Edwared, W. Cundiff et.al—Fundamentals of modern marketing.

Eugene, J. Kelly and William Lazer-Managerial marketing : perspectives and view points.

Frank and Finch—A Concise encyclopedia of management techniques

Grewal, T.S.—Double entry Book keeping.

Iyengar, S.P.—Cost accounting.

Jain, S.P. and Narang. K.L.—Pracitcal problems in advaneed accounting.

James C. Van Horne—Fundamentals of financial management.

Kul Karni, P.V.—Finacial management.

Lal Nigam, B.M. and Sharma, G.L.—Techniques of cost accounting.

Latiff, T.A.A.—The Practice of marketing.

Memoria, C.B. and Joshi, R.L.—Priciples and practice of marketing in India.

Nicholas Dopuch—Accounting data for management decisions.

Pandey, I.M.—Financial management

Philip Kotler—Marketing management : analysis planning implimentation and control.

Rustom S. Daver—Modern marketing management.

Sexena, H.M.—Geography of marketing.

William, E. Thomas—Readings in cost Accounting and budgeting control.

William, F. Schoell—Marketing : Contemporary concepts and practices.

Index

ABC analysis, 153
Accounting of marketing personal, 140-71
  Capital budgeting, 166-69
  Conceptual framework, 140-42
    Accrual basis, 141
    Business entity concept, 140
    Cost concept, 141
    Dual aspect concept, 141
    Going concern concept, 141
    Money measurement, 141
    Realisation concepts, 141
  Cost accounting, 148-55
    ABC analysis, 153
    Accounting for materials, 151
    Cost component, 148
    Cost of production, 150-51
    Cost of sales, 151
    Cost price methods, 153
    Cost sheet, 149
    Cost sheet for the period direct material, 149-50
    Danger line, 152
    Economic ordering quantity, 152
    Highest in first out method, 155
    Market price method, 154
    Maximum level, 151
    Minimum level, 152
    Prime cost, 150
    Recorder level, 152
    Standard price method, 154-55
    Valuation of materials, 153
    VED Analysis, 153
    Work of factory cost, 150
  Financial accounting records, 142-48
    Cash book, 147-48
    Journal, 143
    Ledger, 143
    Purchase book, 146
    Purchase relations book, 147
    Sales book, 146
    Sales return book, 147
    Trading and profit and loss account and balance sheet, 148
    Trial balance, 143-46
  Human resource accounting, 170-71
    Historical cost, 171
    Replacement cost, 171
  Inflation accounting, 169-70
  Marketing research and development accounts, 155-56
    Capitalization method, 156
    Revenue method, 156
  Ratio analysis, 163-66
  Tools for, 156-61
    Application, 158
    Cash flow analysis, 158
    Fund flow analysis, 157
    Items added to net profit, 157
    Items deducted from net profit, 157
    Leverages, 158-61
    Sources, 158
  Value analysis, 161-63
Advertising, 28-32
  Amplified expressiveness, 28
  Case history, 30
  Celebrity, 30
  Children, 31
  Decision on, 30
  Demonstration, 30
  Humorous, 30
  Impersonal, 28
  Media of, 29
  Musical effect in, 31
  Objectives of, 29
  Pervasiveness, 28
  Public presentation, 28
  Requirement of good, 31-32
  Sex appeal, 30
  Technical expertise, 31
  Techniques of, 30

Advertising council of India, 32
American Marketing Association, 25, 135, 140
Antony, Robert, 123
Bill Market Scheme, 72
Business Entity concept, 140
Buyers Credit Scheme, 73-74
CANFIN Homes Ltd., 81
Capital budgeting, 166-69
  Diversification, 167
  Expansion, 166
  Modernisation, 166
  Replacement, 166
  Research and development, 162
  Strategic investment, 167
  Techniques, 162-69
    Average rate of return, 167
    Discounted rate of return method, 169
    Internal rate of return, 167-68
    Net present worth, 168
  Pay back period, 167
    Profitability index, 168-69
Clark, 10
Commercial banks, 72
Consumer finance, 74-83
  Charge account, 76-77
  Credit cards, 82-83
  Hire purchase agreement, 78-79
  Hire vendors account, 79-80
  Instalment credit, 77
  Specialised consumer finance scheme, 80-82
Contact agencies, 66
Cost accounting, 148-55
Cost price methods, 153
Cost volume profit decisions, 102-06
Credit cards, 82-83
Cundiff, Edward W., 25
Debentures, 48-49
Distribution, 23-27
  Channel choice, 24
  Intensity of, 24-25
  Retail, 26
  Retailers classification, 26-27
  Services of wholesalers, 25
  Services to producers, 26
  Services to retailers, 26
  Wholesale, 25
    Classification of, 25
Exim bank, 72-74
  Buyers credit scheme, 73-74
  Exim lines of credit, 74
  For telling, 74
Export Credit Guarantee Corporation of India Ltd., 72-73
Export Credit (Internal subsidy) Scheme, 71
Export marketing financing, 64-74
  Cultural factors, 65
  Geographical/Environment, 65
  Institutions involved in, 71-74
    Commercial banks, 72
    Exim bank, 72
  Post-shipment finance, 71
  Pre-shipment finance, 66-71
    Contact agencies, 66-67
    Developing export accessibility, 67
    Distribution network, 68
    Efforts for exploring export potentials, 66
    Letter of credit, 68-71
    Overseas administrative overhead, 68
    Product designing and development, 67
    Sales promotion, 68
    Storage and warehouses, 67-68
    Workforce management, 68
  Political and demographic, 64
  Socio economic, 65
Financial Accounting records, 142-48
Finance for marketing, 44-83
  Consumer finance, 74-83
  Financing for specific marketing events, 50-74
    For distribution, 55-57
    For product development and positioning, 50-51
      Cash cows, 51
      Dogs, 51
      Star products, 51
    For promotion, 57-68
      Communication related aspects, 58
      Company related aspects, 58
      Competition role, 60
      Consideration for allocation, 59
      Consumer related aspects, 57
      Financial allocation, 58-59

Market related aspects, 57
Position of firm, 60
Product related aspects, 57
Strategy for, 58
Product planning and development, 51-54
Brand positioning, 53-54
Business analysis, 52
Commercialisation, 52-53
Idea generation, 51
Idea screening, 52
Product development, 52
Test marketing, 52
Position in product life cycle, 60-74
Accounting for promotional expenses, 62-64
Financing for export marketing, 64-74
Methods of financial outlay for, 60-62
Long-term financial requirements, 47-50
Debentures, 48-49
Factors determining, 47-48
Functions of, 47
Leasing, 49
Shares, 48
Term loan, 50
Short term financial requirements, 44-47
Extent of requirement, 45
Need for, 44-45
Sources of, 45-47
Accrued expanses and deferred income, 46-47
Advances from customers, 46
Short-term borrowings, 46
Trade credit, 45
Foreign Exchange Regulation Act, 74
GATT, 66
Hire Purchase Act 1972, 78
Hire Purchase Agreement, 78-79
Accounting of purchase and installed, 78-79
Hire Vendors Account, 79
Rate of Interest, 79-80
Specialized consumer finance schemes, 80-82
Home Improvement Loan, 81
Housing Development Finance Corporation Ltd., 81
Huegy, 9
Human Resource Accounting, 170-71
IMF, 66
India Housing and Development Ltd., 82
India Housing Finance Development Ltd., 81
Industrial Credit and Investment Corporation of India, 50, 73
Industrial Development Bank of India, 50
Industrial Finance Corporation, 50
Inflation accounting, 169-70
Instalment credit, 77
Kelly, Eugne, J., 115
Kotler, Philip, 2, 3, 5, 14, 39, 92, 129
Lazer, William, 115
Leasing, 49
Financial, 49
Operating, 49
Letter of credit, 68-71
Back to back, 70
Documentary clean, 69
Fixed credit and revolving credit, 70
Red Clause, 70-71
Revocable and irrevocable, 69
Transferable and non-transferable, 70
Types of, 69
With and without recourse, 70
Leverages, 158-61
Assets, 159
Combined, 160-61
Financial, 159-60
Fixed charges, 160
Operating, 159
Return on investment, 159
Total, 160
Levitt, Theodore, 2
Life Insurance Corporation, 50
Life Insurance Housing Finance Ltd., 88
Long term financial requirements, 47-50
Marginal costing in marketing cost, 89-102
Marketing, 1-13
Concept of, 3-5
Difference in sales and marketing, 3
Environmental conditions for, 5

Evolution of, 1-2
Functions of, 6-11
Need for financial approach, 11-13
Sales concept, 1-2
Marketing audit, 129-34
Approaches and scope of, 130-31
Continuous, 130
Distribution strategy, 132
Elaborate, 129
Internal, 130
Limitations of, 134
Macro environment, 131
Market audit procedure, 132-33
Confirmation, 133
Reporting, 133
Reconciliation, 133
Scanning, 133
Vouching, 133
Market audit programme, 132
Marketing efficiency, 132
Marketing functional, 132
Marketing sales force, 132
Marketing strategy, 131
Merits of, 134
Micro environment, 131
Objectives of, 130-31
Optional, 130
Price strategy, 132
Product strategy, 131
Promotion strategy, 131
Qualification of auditors, 133-34
Marketing cost analysis, 84-106
Cost volume profit decisions, 102-06
Break even analysis, 103
Break even charts, 103-05
Break even point, 103
Margin of safety, 106
Marginal costing in, 89-102
Extension or suspension of distribution outlets, 97-99
Market share decisions, 95
Pricing decisions, 96-97
Product-droop or add decisions, 94-95
Product mix decisions, 92-94
Profitability lend decision, 100-02
Strategic factors, 99-100
Tool cost method, 91-92
Market cost relationship analysis, 86-89
Limitations of, 88-89
Ratio analysis, 87-88
Market cost statement, 85-86
Marketing cost control, 107-39
Marketing finance budget, 120-34
Application of finance, 120
Marketing profitability accounting, 125-28
Allotment of functional expenses, 125
Audit, 129-34
Preparation of accounting statement for, 126-28
Segregation of allotment of functional expenses, 126
Marketing responsibility accounting, 122-25
Process of, 123-24
Pyramid effect of, 124-25
Sales, 120
Zero base market budget, 120-22
Market information system, 134-39
Tools to control activities, 108-20
Budgeting, 108
Budget related cosmetics, 109-10
Cost budget, 114
Functions of based marketing budget, 110
Marketing performance budget-marketing debt, 110-20
Marketing research and development budget, 117-18
Market segment, 113
Production item, 111-12
Production budget, 110-11
Product line based budget, 109
Sales budget, 111
Sales person, 113
Sales promotion budget, 115-17
Time period, 113
Market cost relationship analysis, 86-89
Limitations of, 88-89
Absence of details, 89
In accessible data, 89
Inaccurate details, 89
Lack of standardised cost, 89
Quantification of data, 89
Presence of joint costs, 89
Ratio analysis in relation to marketing, 87-88

Marketing information system, 134-39
- Development of, 136-37
- Flow table, 137-39
  - Advertising response analysis, 139
  - Customer file processing on sample basis, 137
  - Sales commission computation, 139

Marketing mix, 14-43
- Distribution (Place), 23-25
  - Channel choice, 24
  - Intensity of, 24-25
  - Services to wholesalers, 25
  - Wholesale distribution, 25
  - Wholesalers classification, 25
- Packaging, 40-41
- Price, 41-43
  - Cost plus pricing methods, 41-42
  - Marginal cost pricing, 42
  - Pricing for new product, 42-43
- Product, 14-23
  - Factor analysis, 19
  - Image profile analysis, 18-19
  - Product classification, 16-18
    - Based on utility, 16
    - On the basis of shopping habits, 16
    - On the basis of tangibility, 17
    - On the basis of user, 17
    - Product positioning, 17-18
  - Product life cycle, 19-21
    - Decline, 21
    - Growth, 19
    - Maturity, 20
    - Saturation, 20
  - Product mix, 15-16
  - Product planning and development, 21-23
- Promotion, 28-41
  - Advertising, 28-32
  - Public relation, 40
  - Publicity, 39-40
  - Sales promotion, 32-34
  - Selling process/personnel, 35-39
    - Administration of, 37
    - Compensation, 39
    - Control, 39
    - Qualities of, 36-37
    - Recruitment, 37-38

Marketing research and development accounting, 155-56

Market price method, 154

Methods of financial outlays for promotion, 60-62
- Objective task basis, 61-62
- Percentage on sale basis, 61
- Subjective budgeting basis, 61

Mitchell, 9

Money measurement, 141

Packaging, 40-41

Pre-ship finance, 66-71

Preshipment Credit Refinance Facility, 72

Price, 41-43
- Cost plus pricing method, 41-42
- For new product, 42-43
  - High skiming pricing method, 42
  - Low penetration method, 42-43
- Marginal cost processing, 42

Product, 14-15

Product classification, 16-17

Product drop or add decision, 94

Product life cycle, 19-21

Product mix, 15-16

Product mix decisions, 92-94

Product positioning, 17-18

Public relation, 40

Publicity, 39-40

Pyle, 6

Ratio analysis, 163-66
- Benefits of, 163
- Liquidity ratio, 163-64
- Prosprietary ratio, 164-66

Reserve Bank of India,
- Financial support Schemes of, 71-72
  - Bill market scheme, 72
  - Export Credit (Interest subsidy), scheme, 71
  - Preshipment Credit Refinance Facility, 72

Retailers, 26-27

Sales promotion, 32-34

Sales promotion budget, 115-17
- High/medium carry over situation, 115
- Low carry over situation, 115-17
- No carry over situation, 115

Schoell, William F, 5, 28

Selling personnel, 35-39

Administration of, 37
Compensation, 39
Control, 39
Quality of, 36-37
Recruitment, 37-38
Training, 38
Shares, 48
Short term financial requirements, 44-47
Specialized Consumer Finance Schemes, 80-82
Standard price methods, 153-54
Stanton, William J., 5
Still, 25
Storage and ware house, 67-68
Term loan, 50
Trade credit, 145
Value analysis, 161-63
Cost reduction, 162
Objects of, 162-63
Process of, 162
VED Analysis, 153
Wholesalers, 25-26
Classification of, 25
Services to, 26
Zero Base Marketing budget, 120-22